Contemporary Case Studies in School Counseling

Edited by
Marguerite Ohrtman
Erika Heltner

ROWMAN & LITTLEFIELD
Lanham • Boulder • New York • London

Executive Editor: Mark Kerr
Assistant Editor: Courtney Packard
Production Editor: Lara Hahn
Cover Designer: Beth Schlenoff

Credits and acknowledgments of sources for material or information used with permission appear on the appropriate page within the text.

Published by Rowman & Littlefield
An imprint of The Rowman & Littlefield Publishing Group, Inc.
4501 Forbes Boulevard, Suite 200, Lanham, Maryland 20706
https://rowman.com

6 Tinworth Street, London SE11 5AL, United Kingdom

British Library Cataloguing in Publication Information Available

Library of Congress Cataloging-in-Publication Data Available

ISBN 978-1-5381-1803-0 (hardback : alk. paper) | ISBN 978-1-5381-1804-7 (pbk. : alk. paper) | ISBN 978-1-5381-1805-4 (electronic)

∞ ™ The paper used in this publication meets the minimum requirements of American National Standard for Information Sciences Permanence of Paper for Printed Library Materials, ANSI/NISO Z39.48-1992.

To my husband, Nick, and my children, Gabe and Violet.
To my school counseling students of the past, present, and future.
—Marguerite Ohrtman

To all the students with whom I have had the honor of working.
—Erika Heltner

Contents

Preface

This book was created to fill a gap in the training of school counselors. So often in training programs, case study texts are written by those in mental health settings, not actual school counselors. We wanted to hear from real, working school counselors who are navigating complex and multifaceted family and school systems while meeting the social and emotional needs of each individual student in their caseload. We chose to use first-person narrative in order to provide a view into the cognitions, feelings, and behaviors of school counselors as they deal with tough situations in a school setting. We hope that this book serves as a conversation starter for school counselor trainees or young professionals in the counseling field. This book is not intended to model perfect school counseling techniques; rather, we hope to provide an opportunity for readers to explore and analyze authentic cases and challenges faced by school counselors every day. The case studies present many successes but perhaps most useful to the reader are the counselors' moments of honesty and vulnerability presented in these chapters.

We explored six theoretical approaches throughout the chapters: humanist, Adlerian, reality/choice, family systems, solution-focused, and discrimination model supervision theory. These theories were chosen based on the research in the field of school counseling and on our own experiences in using these approaches. In school counseling, we found these theories the most helpful for working with children and adolescents in a school setting. The book is organized based on theory and grade level so readers understand how these theories work when applied to different developmental stages of the students.

There are few recently published school counseling case study texts and none that are written in first person. This book truly guides the reader through the counselor's process, explores the theory and interventions, and applies the American School Counseling Association national model. This text is best suited for school counselor trainees and new school counselors, and we hope that these case studies ignite conversations with colleagues as well as provide an opportunity for the reader to reflect on his/her individual approach. The text challenges readers to not only understand the author's perspective, but also to explore how they would handle the situation if they were in the role of school counselor. Our hope is that readers can explore their own values, beliefs, counseling style, and theoretical approach while reading each chapter.

We recruited school counselors and school counselor educators from across the United States to contribute to this book. We were fortunate to have so many unique and talented voices tell their stories of school counseling and their work with their students. We hope that our readers find that they can immerse themselves into these case studies in order to emerge with new knowledge and perspectives that will guide them in their careers. These real examples provide just a snapshot of the work that school counselors do and are not to be considered the only option for handling the presenting concern. We hope that these case studies start conversations and help school counselors develop into the best school counselors that they can be.

Introduction

The role of school counselors today is multifaceted; school counselors are advocates for students, vital members of the education team, and dynamic leaders in the school system. The general public, including parents, administrators, the media, and community members, often wonders what counselors do on a daily basis. The American School Counselor Association defines a school counselor's role as encompassing three domains: academic achievement, career, and social/emotional development. Counselors, and their efforts within these three domains, help students develop skills to become productive, happy, and healthy individuals as they enter into adulthood.

At the foundation of our work as school counselors is the belief that every person has inherent worth, and this must be the cornerstone of our practice. We must try and see each student for his or her uniqueness and his or her goodness. Even when students exhibit challenging behaviors, we must return to our belief that every student is innately good. Our ability to empathize with each child helps us to see beyond the outward behaviors and fronts. Some of our most fulfilling work comes as a result of patience and steadfast commitment to see all students as having value.

"Humanist psychologists see human nature as good, with an inborn actualizing tendency that drives us toward our highest potential and an organismic valuing process that lead us to prize choices that are good for us and for the peace and harmony of humanity" (Day, 2008). This statement attempts to summarize the humanistic approach, and this theory lies at the very core of school counseling. The concept of self-actualization—a person moving closer and closer to an authentic self—aligns with the work of school counselors as we work with children who are moving toward a better self each and every day. The idea that each of our students has a core of genuine uniqueness attempting to emerge into the world to do good for the self and others sounds idealistic but it's an idea that school counselors embrace. We embrace it because we believe in the power of human connection, and we believe that every child can find academic, social, emotional, and career success if we work alongside our students as they discover their unique strengths.

The counselor is steadfast in positive regard and empathy and remains a stable and trustworthy presence in the life of a student while the relationship serves to empower the child by linking him/her to a more actualized version of him-/herself. The student still has to face his/her own issues alone, but the relationship provides ways to cultivate strength to manage and sometimes fight the circumstances. Counseling is the pursuit to know humanity on all levels and to respect, love, acknowledge, and heal through a connection to and relationship with another human being.

This book provides authentic examples of counselors working to meet the needs of individual students. These chapters are meant to be read in the pursuit of wisdom and in the spirit of developing and evolving the reader's counseling skills. But more importantly, we hope this text introduces realistic scenarios and provides an opportunity for discussion and analysis as future counselors develop and evolve their practice.

REFERENCE

Day, S. (2008). *Theory and design in counseling and psychotherapy*. Boston: Lahaska Press, Houghton Mifflin.

Part I

Humanistic Theory

What is necessary to change a person is to change his awareness of himself.
—Abraham Maslow

Chapters 1 through 3 examine the approach of humanistic theory developed by Abraham Maslow and Carl Rogers. The basis of this theory is that an individual needs to become him- or herself through the process of self-actualization. This focus of the humanistic school of thought is likewise at the core of school counseling. The approach encourages the student to be self-directed, to make their own choices, and to control their actions. School counselors strive to provide the space for students to do this important work and to see the world through the eyes of their students. Finally, school counselors utilize this theoretical approach to be empathic and to help their students reach their full potential.

For the first three chapters, school counselors describe not only their work with their students, but also their own journey of self-actualization as a school counselor. The counselors approach the situation with compassion, understanding, and a clear awareness of who they are as school counselors. All chapters discuss the personal work that the school counselors exhibited to challenge their own biases, as well as how they explored their own feelings of discomfort. In the third chapter, the author reminds us to be mindful of these biases and to explore these feelings of discomfort.

Chapter One

Liam

This case study occurred in a large metropolitan school district in which the school counselor was the only counselor for more than 650 students. This elementary school counselor was new to the counseling profession and still developing her counseling style and had been with the school for three years at the time of this case study.

As you read this case study, look for the following:

- The counselor's intention and how that leads the sessions
- Humanistic counseling interventions and strategies
- The role of values in the counseling relationship

CASE STUDY INTRODUCTION

My family and friends usually understand what high school counselors do, and most have at least an idea of what middle school counseling looks like. Elementary counseling, however, is plagued with misconceptions. It is not comforting small children when they scrape a knee, or singing "Kumbaya," or hanging out in your office all day.

When asked what I do, I like to say, "What *don't* I do?" Admittedly, this response doesn't address the question—even if it provides a small sense of satisfaction. What I really mean is that I am always on the go, and my job varies from day to day, moment to moment. I am in classrooms teaching lessons on social skills, career options, and many other topics. I run groups during my lunch hour in which I work with students facing hard transitions like family change, loss, and social skills. I also counsel individual students on their varying needs, which can include issues such as caring for younger siblings (while themselves children), homelessness, and even abuse. Most

people I encounter are startled to learn that young children face these problems. Elementary counseling can be intense work, as children can indeed
have intense life problems.

However, the resiliency of the students that I work with amazes me every
day. With a humanistic theoretical lens, I try to approach each student as an
individual. I believe that all children have a story to share and have their own
experiences that shape their world. I also know that I have my own experiences that shape how I encounter each student, group, and classroom. Understanding the role of my own values is important and oftentimes difficult as I
strive to be open and receptive to all my students.

With children this young, it is easy to try to fix the problem they are
presenting. I often think that if I could just tell them what to do, we could
have their issue solved in minutes! However, that is not what counseling is
about, and that is not the type of counselor I want to be. When students have
control, especially elementary students, there is ownership of their goals and
a commitment to their plan, which simply would not exist if I were to push
my plan. I debate a lot with my principal about this, as he struggles to
understand the concept of not telling students what to do. He argues that it
saves time and we can avoid all the "wishy-washy" stuff. I usually laugh at
that and remind him that I can get results my way, too. Although we don't
see eye-to-eye on our approach, he does respect the work I do—probably
because he sees those results.

However, one of the struggles of my job is that I don't always have an
opportunity to meet each student individually. I am responsible for adminis-
tering state testing every other month, leaving even less time for one-on-one
meetings. I often see students only when I am in a reactive state, not a
proactive mind-set. Children are referred to me by teachers, administrators,
other support personnel, and, once in a while, a concerned parent or guardian. Although I work very hard to get to know each student, the task feels
impossible at times. Often, I meet students only when they are in crisis or, in
the case of Liam, when they move into our school district. As part of my role,
I meet with all students who transfer to our school, introducing them to our
building and helping them adjust to their new community.

INCIDENT

As an elementary counselor, I am used to disheveled children. They usually
are the ones who put up a fight with their parent or guardian about brushing
their hair or teeth, bathing, or what they want to wear. When eight-year-old
Liam was escorted to my office, I saw a new level of disheveled. His hair
was dirty, so dirty that dry shampoo couldn't disguise that he hadn't washed
in who knows how long. He was wearing worn gray sweatpants, his red shirt

looked like he slept in it, and I am pretty sure he didn't have socks on with his untied shoes. He stood there looking at the ground and away from me as if trying to go unnoticed.

"This is Liam," his teacher announced. "He hasn't been doing any work for me and he won't bring homework home. Can you work on him?" She wasn't known for her subtlety.

"Hi, Liam," I said. "I'm so glad that you came to visit."

His teacher nodded at me and scurried off, dismissing the possibility of any further explanation as to why she brought him to me. She seemed to think I could "fix" the problem. Although I wish I had a magic wand to materialize homework and help children be productive in class, most problems like these aren't because the child is lazy or unwilling to do the work. There is usually something else going on.

Liam continued to stand in the doorway. He was halfway through second grade, but we had met briefly just a few weeks before when he transferred to our school. He had been an only child until a new baby brother arrived this year; his mom remarried and they moved to her new husband's home in our school district. When we'd met a few weeks prior, Liam was a completely different child than the one who stood so awkwardly in my office door now.

Five weeks ago, Liam walked in, a bright-eyed child with a shy smile, holding his mom's hand. She was juggling holding his hand and the baby carrier. The baby was crying, as babies do, but Liam's mom looked stressed as she weakly smiled at me. Liam plopped right down in one of my office chairs; she struggled to drop her purse and swing the carrier to soothe the new baby.

"Welcome to our school. I am the school counselor here and really glad that we could meet," I said, directing my attention to the excited little boy. "You must be Liam." I reached out my hand to shake his.

He shook it vigorously. "This is my mom and my brother, Nyx. We just moved here from Mobile." He was so excited to be here that it was radiating off of his body. His mom, on the other hand, looked like she was hoping to drop him off, as she couldn't quite get settled. There was an uneasiness about her: she was looking around my office, shifting in her chair, and avoiding eye contact with me.

"Liam is here to start second grade. You should have his information already. Is there anything else you need from me?" she asked tensely.

Liam continued to smile at me and look around my office. I'd had the opportunity to chat with his former counselor and she'd had no concerns about him; indeed, he seemed now a happy, confident kid.

I politely smiled at them both. "I did receive his information," I said, "and we are so glad to have you here. I can take him to his new classroom to meet his teacher if you need to go. Do you have the information for busing for after school or will you be picking him up each day?"

"He can ride the bus. . . . Do I need to sign for that?" she asked abruptly. I quickly grabbed some paperwork from my new student folder and shared it with her.

"You can fill this out in the main office on your way out today. Are you sure you wouldn't like to see Liam's new classroom?" I prodded.

"I don't have time. Liam, I will see you after school," she stated matter-of-factly. With that, she stood up, turned her back, and hustled out with the baby before I had time to shake her hand.

I turned to Liam. "Let's go meet your new teacher and introduce you to some of your new classmates." We walked out together and he started to chatter excitedly.

"Do you have a soccer team here? Do you get to roller skate in gym? I like soccer a lot and play every Saturday with my friends at my old school," he shared.

"We do have soccer here, and I know a lot of other children in your class play soccer at recess. I am sure you will make a lot of friends here," I assured him, relieved that whatever his mom was going through, he seemed secure enough to weather this transition.

A few short weeks later, here was Liam back in my office staring at the floor. I moved my chair a little closer to his, not to the point where our knees were touching, but close enough to let him know I was there.

"Liam, I didn't recognize you right away today when you came in. You look a little different to me," I dropped lightly—a polite way, I hoped, to point out his appearance and to see if I could find out what was going on. "When we met a few weeks ago, you were so excited about being at our school and we had so much fun talking about all your favorite things, like soccer and basketball.

He stared at the floor.

"You look like you might be feeling a little sad today," I said, hoping for a response. He gave me nothing to work with his nonverbals.

I persisted and said, "Maybe you don't want to talk right now?" Still no response. I'd have to try a different approach, I thought to myself.

"Liam, I think we should just sit here together. Whenever you are ready to talk or if I can do anything, just let me know. I am glad just to be here with you." I thought I could create a safe space for him. Usually, silence is unheard of with eight-year-olds, unless they are playing with technology. Being present with elementary students can be hard since I have such a large caseload; with so many students, it is a luxury to be able just to sit and completely focus on one student. However, with Liam, this felt like the best choice.

We sat there in silence for about three minutes, though I am sure it felt a lot longer to him. I wanted to allow him to take the lead and not feel like I was pestering him with questions. He finally looked up at me and said, "I'm hungry."

I quickly responded, "I have some snacks," and opened my super-secret snack drawer, which, sadly, I use more often than I would like.

"What looks good to you?" I asked. Although his response was not the one I was hoping for, he did finally speak to me.

He grabbed a giant bag of Swedish Fish that I'd forgotten was in there. Probably not the best choice for him, but I thought to myself that this wasn't the battle I wanted to pick today with Liam. He started to inhale the candy and I quietly sat there watching.

"How is it?" I asked.

"Good," he responded.

I was wondering if maybe, with a full stomach, he would start to tell me more about what was going on when there was a knock at my door. The school social worker was standing there peering through my door window with a curious look on her face. I nodded at her and she motioned for me to join her in the hallway.

"Liam, I will be right back," I said.

I met her in the doorway and quietly moved her outside of my office to be out of earshot of Liam.

"Everything okay?" I asked.

"I heard you were meeting with Liam, and I wanted to follow up with you about him," she said. *Wow, news really spreads fast here*, I thought, but then remembered that the teacher who brought Liam was good friends with the social worker.

"He and I are just getting to know each other," I explained. "He hasn't shared much, but is there anything I need to know?" I have a good relationship with the social worker and we have been able to collaborate together often.

"I know that he has been coming in looking worse and worse," she shared. "Some of the other kids are saying things about his smell and appearance." I quickly nodded to confirm that I'd noticed the change.

"His mom won't answer when I call and his stepdad isn't even listed in the information we have on him. I don't think he has a caseworker but maybe he should," she continued. She and I often have made calls to protective services about students, but I wasn't sure that was the case yet with Liam. It is hard not to jump to conclusions, especially when the child presents himself the way Liam did today.

"Thank you for coming down, but I want to see if I can make some progress with him today," I said. I wanted to be careful to avoid gossiping with her when I could try talking to Liam directly, who still was sitting quietly in my office.

She nodded like she understood. "I will follow up with you later."

I stepped back inside and found that Liam had resumed his position: head down, staring at his shoes.

"Sorry I had to step out there for a minute, Liam. How are you feeling now after those Swedish Fish?" I asked, hoping that it might be easy to get him to respond to me now. He shrugged his shoulders. It was not going to be *that* easy.

"Liam, do you know why your teacher brought you down today?" I really hate asking this question, as most elementary students either have no idea or give an absurd reason they have concocted.

"I am not sure. She seemed mad, but I didn't do anything in class," he said quietly.

"It sounds like maybe she is concerned about you. Do you think maybe that could be it?" I said hopefully.

"I don't know. I don't like it here," Liam said.

He looked at me like I was not understanding. I thought about my next words carefully. I didn't want to continue to challenge his conceptions, so I thought I would ask about home.

"How are things at home? Are you enjoying your new brother Nyx?" I asked. With his appearance having changed so much, I wanted to make sure I asked about his safety at home.

"Things are fine. I just hate it here," he said again.

"How are you liking your new home?" I persisted, hoping that he would give me some clues to what his home life was like.

"It's bigger than our last house and I got to decorate my room," he shrugged.

"Well, that sounds really great. Are Mom and Nyx home with you after school?" I explored.

"Yeah, she meets me at the bus stop. Nyx cries a lot. Mom says he is kinky." I kept a straight face and hoped he meant "colicky."

"That must be tough. So Nyx cries a lot?" I reflected back to him.

"Oh, yeah. *All* the *time!*" he emphasized. "Mom says I need to be good and not be loud after school. She gets mad when I wake the baby."

"I bet that it is hard to be quiet, but I am sure your mom appreciates it," I said. "Does Mom help you get dressed in the morning, Liam?"

"No, she says to put something on and then I have to run to the bus stop," he admitted.

"Got it. So you get ready pretty quickly in the morning and don't check in with Mom before you leave." I thought to myself that maybe a call home to Mom might help this situation. From what Liam was sharing, it sounded like she was overwhelmed and perhaps Liam's hygiene wasn't her primary concern. Understandable, yet if his hygiene improved, he might be able to make friends a little easier. I wrote myself a quick sticky note on my desk to call home and check in with his mom.

"So tell me about how school has been going since we last talked?" I questioned.

"I don't have any of my friends here. No one likes to play with me and my teacher always looks at me weird," he said matter-of-factly. "I had friends in Mobile. Everyone was way nicer. My teacher didn't yell and everyone played soccer." As he shared this, I started to think about how hard it is to be the new kid in school. I wondered how much of what I was seeing now was because of his new surroundings.

I wanted to get a clearer picture of what he was experiencing, so I asked, "How does Ms. Everett look at you weird?" I was hoping that maybe we could connect through the use of humor.

He scrunched up his nose and curled his lips up like a rabid dog. I laughed out loud. "Well, that is quite the face! I hope she doesn't really look that way at you," I said, "but I'm glad that you are telling me that you are having a hard time connecting with your teacher and other students. It sounds like you might be feeling a little lonely here at school."

"I just hate it here." Again, with the strong language of "hate."

"That hurts my heart, Liam, to hear that you are so unhappy. If you had to name the worst thing about being here at school, what would you say?" I questioned further.

"I don't have any friends and no one likes me," he said, becoming exasperated.

"Friends can be really tough to make when you are new. Can you tell me who you sit by at lunch?"

"I don't sit with anyone. Everyone here doesn't like me," he said. I noted the extreme language he was using with "any" and "everyone." Because I wanted to understand what this looked like for him, I pressed: "There's not one person who likes you in this school?"

"No," he said.

"Okay, so tell me about your day here at school. When you first arrive, what happens?" I asked, hoping to get more information about what else may be causing these behaviors.

"I get here and sit by myself. No one comes to talk to me and no one wants to do anything with me," he replied.

"Have you tried talking to anyone when you arrive?" I probed.

"I tried, but they didn't like me," he sighed.

"Who did you try to talk to? Can you tell me what happened?" I asked.

"It was at recess. I asked Ian to play soccer with me and he said no. I got mad and kicked the ball. It hit the ceiling in the gym and I got in trouble," he said angrily. "It's his fault for making me mad."

"Liam, that sounds like a really bad situation all around," I empathized. "You were mad at Ian because you got in trouble during recess when you were angry with him. Did you try to talk to your teacher about it afterward?"

He looked at me and said, "No, everyone here sucks."

I smiled at him. "I am sorry that you are feeling that way, Liam. I don't think everyone here is like that. Have you tried talking with any other students?" I didn't address the word "sucks," since, frankly, I have heard a lot worse come out of some students' mouths and didn't think it was worth addressing today.

"I don't wanna talk to anyone. I just hate being here," he said. *At least he is being consistent regarding his feelings about school*, I thought.

"When I first met you, Liam, I liked you right away. I think that maybe being new here has been hard and that maybe the other students might need a little help getting to know you. Would you be willing to give them a chance to get to know you?" I asked.

"I don't know. It's hard," he said with a large tear starting to form in his right eye.

"I know it can be really hard being new and having a lot of new changes. I want to help you if you would let me. Would you be willing to let me help you, Liam, with your teacher and making friends?" I asked.

"I don't know. Maybe," he said.

"We could meet each week to talk about how things are going, and if you want, you could bring a new friend with you to meet with me. We could play some games together so that you get to know some different students in your class. What do you think about that idea?" I asked.

"I don't know. Maybe . . . but what if I wanted to bring two people?" he asked with a hopeful smirk.

"Well, let's start with one new friend this week and see how it goes. Sound fair?" I asked with a smile.

"Okay. I guess so," he said, looking up at me with a small twinkle in his eye, as if he was already thinking about whom he would ask.

"I think we should talk to Ms. Everett and your mom about the homework situation. Ms. Everett said that you weren't doing your homework. Can you tell me about that?" I inquired.

"I always forget it at home," he said quietly.

"Hmm . . . maybe I can talk to your mom about it on the phone and see if we can help remind you to bring it. Does that sound okay—that I call to talk to Mom?" I was already planning to call home, but I prefer to give students notice so that they are not taken aback when they hear that I have called. I wanted to check in with Mom about his appearance and was guessing that with her help we could solve a few of Liam's problems with an earlier alarm and a quick check-in before he left each morning.

"Okay, am I in trouble?" he asked.

"No, Liam. You are definitely not in trouble," I said, smiling. "I am just going to talk to Mom to see if we can help you get to school with your homework. Sound like a plan?"

"Sure," he said.

"I have one more idea for you, too, Liam. I have students who meet each week in a few groups that I think you might like being part of. I have one group that helps students to make friends and to learn to talk about when we get mad or upset. Would you be interested in learning more about this group?" I offered.

"Maybe. Would I get to come to see you for lunch? I know some kids get to come here for lunch," he inquired.

"Yes, you would get to come here to talk with me and other students. Should we plan on that this week?" I asked.

"Okay," he said with that same sheepish grin I saw five weeks ago.

For the next month, I met with Liam individually and he even came to group the last week of the month. His hygiene started to get a little better, although I could tell when he was having a bad day based on his appearance. After meeting with Liam, I also followed up with his teacher to share with her that we were going to start meeting and that we had started a plan to help him improve at school. Liam tells me that she is nicer to him now, though she still can be really cranky. When I see him outside at recess now, he usually has one or two friends that he is playing with and he is starting to present more like the happy, excited child I met in my office on his first day of school.

CASE DISCUSSION

Using a humanistic counseling lens compelled me to explore Liam beyond what he'd been referred to me for, his academic abilities. I wanted to explore his self-development, as he had quickly declined since starting at our school. Humanistic counseling in theory should explore the child's scope for self-development, as well as choice, freedom, and creativity (Scholl & Brady-Amoon, 2014). As Liam's counselor, I wanted to consider his needs and purpose as we looked to solving his current problem.

When I first met his mother, I found myself judging her and now I was judging Liam because he appeared not well-cared for and neglected. I felt triggered by Liam's appearance, as it reminded me of a student I had during my internship. It was my first call to child protective services and the child was removed from the home. That student reminded me a lot of Liam and I think I made the mistake of jumping to a lot of conclusions during that first interaction with Liam. I struggled a lot after making that first mandated report and struggled to understand how families could be so neglectful of their children. I also need to always check in with my own values and know that no matter what socioeconomic status a family is, children can be neglected and hurt. Every family has a story and I need to be cautious that I don't impose my own values and stereotypes on Liam and his family. Although I am not proud of these misconceptions, I knew I needed to name them and move forward to better serve Liam.

When I first met his mom, I was taken aback and upset that she didn't stay to meet his teacher on that first day. I was still holding on to this when I was meeting with him. I was making assumptions based on one interaction.

In addition to being open, I wanted to be sure that my goals were not *my* goals but rather goals that Liam wanted and were achievable. Oftentimes humanistic counselors may develop their own goals without considering the goals of their clients (Bohart, 2003). Sometimes school counselors get into a rhythm of trying simply to "fix" the child and get him or her back to class. This "fix" usually meant talking with the student briefly and getting them back to class as quickly as possible without truly exploring the actual problem. For example, I didn't want to "fix" Liam, but rather to help him become more self-directed. By slowing down and listening to him, I was able to understand what was going on from his perspective. I needed to explore with him what obstacles were preventing him from moving toward his life goals. Developmentally, Liam's "life goals" consisted of feeling a sense of belonging.

Although he never stated that he wanted to make friends, I assumed that was part of his presenting problem. I thought that exploring how he could make friends would help him feel more comfortable at school and help him develop a sense of belonging. With this age it is difficult to refrain from being too directive with the students, especially in the school setting where most interactions with students are brief.

Finally, I wanted to consider the American School Counseling Association national model in terms of my delivery of services. My approach was to provide him options through group counseling or individual counseling. The American School Counseling Association national model explores students through three domains: academic, career, and emotional/social (ASCA, 2012). Liam was brought to me by his teacher because he was not performing academically. However, the reason he was struggling with his schoolwork was because he was not feeling connected to school, his teacher, or his classmates. I explored his emotional/social domain in the session, with the hopes that working on this domain would resolve the issue in the other. In addition, I planned to connect with his guardian at home and with his teacher about getting his completed homework to school.

DISCUSSION QUESTIONS

1. How might a counselor's personal biases play a role in interactions with students, families, and other staff members?

2. With a humanistic approach, what interventions could the school counselor have attempted with Liam?
3. What next steps would you take when working with Liam? How might the school counselor have connected more with him?

REFERENCES

American School Counselor Association. (2012). ASCA national model: A framework for school counseling programs (3rd ed.). Alexandria, VA: Author.

Bohart, A. C. (2003). Person-centered psychotherapy. In A. S. Gurman & S. B. Messer (Eds.). *Essential psychotherapies: Theory and practice* (2nd ed., pp. 107–48). New York, NY: Guilford Press.

Scholl, D. C. R., & Brady-Amoon, P. (2014). Humanistic counseling process, outcomes and research. *Journal of Humanistic Counseling, 53,* 218–39.

Wright, R. J. (2012). *Introduction to school counseling.* Thousand Oaks, CA: Sage Publications.

Chapter Two

Sarah

When I share with friends that I'm a middle school counselor, I usually am confronted with a cringe, followed by raised eyebrows, and then something like, "Wow, how's that?" or "That must be exhausting." It's not surprising that my peers respond in this way; we all have memories of the social awkwardness, mood swings, and frustrations that come with young adolescence. Most of us roll our eyes at the thought of our thirteen-year-old selves and shake our heads in relief that those days are long gone. It's safe to assume that we were not our best selves at this point in our lives, and for this reason, humanistic counseling is absolutely imperative in middle school counseling. Middle school kids can be headstrong, irrational, moody, argumentative, impulsive, rebellious, and at the same time, insecure, vulnerable, and silly. For this reason, school counselors working with middle school students need to believe wholeheartedly in Carl Rogers's unconditional positive regard (Rogers, 1951). Even when students are at their worst, it is the job of the school counselor to see the good in them and build on this as the counseling relationship is formed.

Middle school students are going through rapid physical changes, including growth spurts and an increase in sexual thoughts and feelings. In addition, their cognitive development is shifting from concrete operational thinking to formal operational thinking, which means that students are moving from thinking in concrete terms to more abstract thought. Middle schoolers progress from inductive reasoning—drawing generalized conclusions based on specific incidents—to deductive reasoning—drawing specific conclusions from abstract concepts using logic. This impacts our work as school counselors, since middle school students fluctuate between these two types of reasoning.

In addition, the definition of self and an integration of this self into a larger social context becomes central to the existence of middle school students. They want autonomy but remain dependent on caregivers and adults in their lives. Through all this, they still are concerned about how their peers view them, and these relationships are the most important in their lives. In an attempt to develop a sense of independence, young adolescents often resist authority and focus on peer relationships as a way of fulfilling social needs. The imaginary audience made up of their peers is also characteristic of middle school students; they often make decisions based on what others will think of them even if there is no immediate audience.

Humanist counselors assert that people develop in a positive manner in a healthy counseling environment. A middle school counselor providing a healthy environment is genuine, accepting, caring, and empathic. The counselor reflects the student's feelings as well as details related in sessions. Reflection serves to facilitate a deep understanding of the self and a validation of the self, which can lead to more positive choices and self-acceptance. And if the counselor reflects an emotion incorrectly, the student is presented with an opportunity to clarify and therefore solidify an even deeper understanding of the self.

In order to help students develop a better sense of self, school counselors relying on humanist techniques work in the "here and now." This is when school counselors can often facilitate the most positive change with students. Developmentally, middle school students are constantly in the here and now; thinking futuristically is difficult. When utilizing a humanistic approach, developing a positive relationship with the student is essential. This relationship provides the foundation for healthy confrontation, which can be the impetus for positive changes in behavior. Confrontation can be uncomfortable for counselors but effective as seen in the following case study.

Finally, the goal of the humanist counselor is to help students develop an effective process for internal evaluation as well as to develop an ability to trust themselves. The hope is that through unconditional positive regard and an empathic relationship, the student will build a strong sense of self and develop a willingness to grow positively and ultimately embrace and display the ideal self, resulting in congruence between the self and the way the child lives his or her life. The school counselor serves as a guide or facilitator through this process. The counselor is not directive, but rather a supportive part of the change process.

As you read this case study, look for the following:

- Humanistic techniques and strategies used in the school counseling session
- Counseling methods that allow for compassion while still holding the student accountable

- The student's avoidant behavior and secondary gains
- The role of the relationship in school counseling

CASE STUDY INTRODUCTION

The following case study relates the story of Sarah, an eighth-grade student struggling with anxiety, and the positive relationship I fostered with her using humanist techniques, among other approaches, as a new school counselor.

INCIDENT

I immediately noticed Sarah's Vans slip-ons because I had the exact same ones. I didn't say anything at the time, but I took note. She was in my office two weeks before her first day of sixth grade because her mother thought a visit with me, her school counselor, and a tour of the school might ease her anxiety, but I suspected the visit was an effort to ease her mother's anxiety just as much as Sarah's.

Sarah was dressed sharply, precociously in fact, in distressed skinny jeans, a t-shirt that read, "Yeah Boyeee," and a gray cardigan sweater despite the sweltering heat outside. I was pretty sure she was already sporting her new school clothes. Her hair was tied up in a tight ponytail, and her build was slight but athletic, like a gymnast. Her brown eyes darted around my office, her hands neatly tucked under her thighs, and her leg bounced rapidly and rhythmically reminding me of a wind-up toy. As neatly and thoughtfully put together as Sarah was, her mother was disheveled and haphazard, wearing loose-fitting jeans and an oversized, faded sweater with her graying hair piled on top of her head in a loose bun. Her eyes, tired but acutely alert, fixed on me as she detailed Sarah's "eccentricities," as she called them.

Her mother laughed nervously as she described Sarah's habit of reorganizing her room compulsively and looked to Sarah for affirmation, "Right Sar?" Sarah looked at the floor and smiled uncomfortably without saying anything and continued to bounce her leg. Her mother talked about Sarah in the third person, detailing the behaviors she'd already explained to me in a previous phone conversation, and I decided to interrupt and suggested we take a tour of the building.

I'd gotten a glimpse into the dynamic between Sarah and her mother and didn't want to force Sarah to listen as her mother described highly personal details about Sarah's struggles. She appeared relieved by the chance to escape something—her mother, me, my office—I wasn't sure which, but she clearly wanted to flee. I was hoping she'd see my efforts to align myself with her, to let her know I felt her embarrassment and discomfort, to let her know I was her advocate.

During this initial meeting I also learned that Sarah's seventeen-year-old sister was in treatment for substance use and her stepfather was inconsistently managing his alcoholism. Additionally, Sarah's mother had endured years of physical abuse from Sarah's biological father; the abuse, according to Sarah's mother, began a few months after Sarah's birth and continued until she was eight, when Sarah's mother and father divorced. Even though Sarah wasn't abused by her father, I inferred that the emotional toll of witnessing the violence was profound and certainly significant in Sarah's case, even if Sarah didn't realize it.

In fifth grade, Sarah was diagnosed with generalized anxiety disorder, and her elementary school subsequently evaluated her for a 504 plan, which included twenty-seven accommodations ranging from "teacher will speak to Sarah about problematic behaviors privately" to "teachers will not call on Sarah without prearranging." Sarah's fifth-grade teacher described Sarah as "having extreme perfectionist tendencies" and also as "prone to give up or become 'sassy' when things were difficult." I worried at the sheer number of accommodations and hoped we could meet her needs in the new and much different setting of middle school.

According to her 504 plan, she was to see me weekly to "check in" regarding homework, behavior, and anxiety management, but every week, she would avoid coming to my office during her set appointment, and I would have to retrieve her from class with a phone call or by walking to her classroom. I took a person-centered approach with her and tried sentence starters, drawing, journaling, reading short stories, directly addressing the resistance, but none of my attempts seemed to move the therapeutic relationship forward. She remained guarded.

During the course of Sarah's sixth- and seventh-grade years, Sarah and I slowly developed a relationship that, for the most part, remained superficial. We were getting to know one another carefully, me asking her easy questions. As long as I didn't delve into her struggles with anxiety, she slowly began to talk more easily about superficial topics like shoes, a subject we both liked. So when she asked me if Vans were popular when I was in middle school, I took this as a positive sign; perhaps she was curious about me, who I'd been as a middle school kid, who I was now.

I responded, "I think they were more popular with skater kids, but not everyone—at least not the girls. I think we wore Keds. Do you know what those are? Are those even around anymore?"

She laughed and assured me that, yes, they were around, though not as cool as Vans or Chuck Taylors. She continued to probe. "So you wore Keds?" she asked.

"Yep, but now I'm more into Vans," I smiled and eyed my silver slip-ons.

She followed up. "What kind of a kid were you in middle school?" she asked, looking down at her own shoes, "Like, were you sporty or a goody-goody?"

I laughed. "I guess I was kind of sporty," I said. "But I don't think anyone would have called me a goody-goody."

She laughed. "Yeah, right," she said, rolling her eyes. "I'm sure you were in detention every week." Her inquiries seemed to be probing me to see if she could trust that I would not judge her if she shared more of herself with me, perhaps a part of herself that didn't fit into the "perfect student" image she constructed up until this point.

Sarah certainly had a Type A personality, and I hoped that this was a healthy coping mechanism for a tumultuous home life. I found myself in awe of her meticulously scribed planner, where she artistically kept an account of how she would spend every second of her day. The final entry read, "Lights out." It was curious but not completely abnormal that she managed her world like this, and it wasn't out of the ordinary that Sarah never uttered a word about her home life in our sessions other than to describe the new paint color or bedding she chose for her bedroom. I've worked with many kids with highly dysfunctional home lives who often settle into the safety of compartmentalization that the school day offers them. Often, I encourage students to organize their experiences into two compartments, home life and school life, as a way—often the *only* way—to manage chaos and succeed in school despite despairing life situations. Establishing boundaries between the two worlds provides such students relief from traumatic home environments and allows them to prosper in a healthy school environment.

I thought that maybe Sarah was in this way effectively steering herself into stability despite her highly unstable and traumatic childhood. It clearly was not without great effort on her part: in our weekly meetings she deflected questions, kept moving (literally, at all times—pacing, tapping, fidgeting), and stayed under the radar. Still, during her first two years of middle school Sarah managed to make it through, maintaining the façade that everything was under control.

But in eighth grade things changed. She hid in the bathroom during classes, told teachers to "f-off," sprinted away from the principal, and when she'd exhausted herself by lashing out, she sobbed and rocked back and forth in my office, face hidden in her hands behind a thick curtain of hair, and then would refuse to return to school for days.

Her mother shook her head. "This is what I've been talking about," she said, with a hint of "I told you so"—relieved, no doubt, that we were finally seeing the Sarah she saw at home.

In those moments when Sarah was crying in my office, she wouldn't talk, wouldn't make eye contact, wouldn't accept even a Kleenex in the way of human interaction, and I found myself feeling helpless. She was inconsolable, and all that I could do was to be with her in her pain, to provide empathy and to allow her to feel this pain in a safe space. Sarah's grip was loosening; she was tiring and looking for another way to regain control. The mosaic of family dysfunction, trauma, peer pressure, academic pressure, adolescence, clinically diagnosed anxiety, and a fierce desire to rise above it all was too much for Sarah; she couldn't incorporate all of these pieces into a sensical design, but she seemed to be trying to manage her inner world by rejecting—smashing to dust—every part of her life except for peer acceptance. Developmentally, this made sense.

Sarah was trying to "save face" socially, and this meant staging a revolt against authority figures who were asking Sarah to remain in class, not knowing that leaving class was the only mechanism she had to manage her anxiety. She was struggling profoundly with her inner world, and learning math, completing an essay, or studying for a test became too much for her. The pressure she put on herself to be a straight-A student combined with the enormous amount of emotional strife she was enduring at home became overwhelming. She couldn't verbalize this nor did she want to share this with me or her teachers. Instead of admitting that she was overwhelmed by academic expectations and terrified that she may appear vulnerable or worse— fail to maintain her outer persona—she pushed back at anyone who she might disappoint. By becoming defiant, she was choosing to take on a rebellious persona rather than to appear weak.

Although I had a glimpse into Sarah's vulnerability, teachers and other school staff did not. Sarah was flippant, shockingly offensive, oppositional, and even aggressive, but when she crumpled into her chair in my office, she was fragile, scared, and broken. And even though Sarah let me see her when she was vulnerable, I never saw this as a conscious decision to open up to me; she simply couldn't hold herself together any longer. But perhaps it was a conscious decision: she felt safe enough in my office to fall apart. During these vulnerable moments when she sat in my office, she remained closed off, not wanting to talk about the source of her despair. She muttered over and over again, "I just want to go home." The next day, when I tried to reflect with her, looking to identify triggers or a pattern or to discuss ways to self-soothe when her anxiety was escalating, she blamed the teachers, calling them "control freaks" or "annoying" and resisted looking inward.

Subsequently, Sarah was finding herself in the principal's office or serving detention on a regular basis, and in turn, finding herself in the company of other students who shared similar coping mechanisms for similarly troubling inner and outer experiences. And in these new relationships, Sarah seemed to find some solace. These new kids accepted her and even provided Sarah an opportunity to be the one providing support rather than the one always in need of support. Sarah seemed to be testing me as she described her new friends, telling me of their rebellious behaviors. I guessed that she thought I would discourage her from hanging out with these friends, but I did my best to refrain from saying anything that she might interpret as advice. As long as she was safe, I was going to listen and reflect her feelings of acceptance and let her know that no matter whom she chose to hang out with, I would remain a constant.

Sarah was now taking an antidepressant to manage her symptoms, and despite several conversations with her mother about seeking additional therapeutic support outside of school, Sarah's mother resisted. She resisted, not because she didn't believe it would be helpful, but because Sarah flatly refused to go. Once, her mother had gotten her to the office of a psychologist, but Sarah refused to get out of the car. Her mother wasn't ready to engage in this battle again, and Sarah's struggles escalated midyear during eighth grade.

On a clear, frigid day in January, I found Sarah, now in eighth grade, sitting at a table in the hall, her hair lit up by the winter sunlight streaming in behind her, headphones on, intently focused on her laptop, leg bouncing rapidly. She was no longer the sharply dressed, highly manicured preteen I'd met two years ago. Sarah was wearing the same clothes she'd been wearing the day before and was disheveled and haphazardly put together, which was unusual for her.

She was supposed to be in algebra, and her teacher had called to see if she was in my office. She'd been avoiding algebra class regularly since the day her teacher called the nurse to escort Sarah to the bathroom because the teacher hadn't believed she truly needed to use the restroom. The teacher was right. Sarah didn't need to use the bathroom, but for some reason, she needed to leave the class. My job as her counselor was to help Sarah see what she was avoiding and help her find a way to address it, allowing her to remain in her classes. We tried a range of cognitive behavioral therapy (CBT) techniques like self-talk and reframing but these didn't seem to help Sarah overcome the anxiety, and avoidance was becoming her go-to coping mechanism. Not surprisingly, the assignments piled up, teachers became more impatient, and the anxiety increased.

I walked over to Sarah's sunlit space and sat in a chair across from her. I simply said, "Hi." She looked up from her laptop and said, "Hi." Just that morning, we'd discussed her "plan," and this wasn't a part of it, although I wondered if mandating her to sit in a sunlit corner would in fact help her mental health. A little vitamin D each day couldn't hurt and might have more impact than anything we'd tried up to this point.

After a brief glance up at me, she lowered her eyes again to her computer screen. I then presumed, "So I'm guessing the plan we talked about this morning has a flaw." One of the corners of her mouth twitched but she didn't look up. I continued, "This is a great spot. I just want to curl up here and take a little nap. Do you think that I would get fired if I did that?" She broke into a tiny smile. "I'm okay with you working here," I said, "but I think you forgot a crucial step in the plan. What step do you think I'm referring to?" The minute I asked that last question, I regretted it. My adolescent self hated it when adults asked me to recite established rules in order to entrap myself.

So I wasn't surprised when she rolled her eyes and then spit out at me, "I know, I know, I need to come tell you I need a break, but if I come tell you I need a break, you'll make me go back to class. Why can't I just be here?" Her 504 plan allowed for her to take five-minute breaks and return to class after using her calming strategies.

I knew that to engage in an argument was futile. However, Sarah was open to talking, and I decided to seize this sunny moment and see if I could learn more about why she was "acting out." Since she'd started her antianxiety medication, there were more moments when she opened up about how her mind worked, which was promising, but these moments were fleeting and also dependent on the regularity with which she took her medication. "What is it about algebra that's causing you to conscientiously object?" I asked. She looked at me, one eyebrow up, annoyed at my choice of words. I rephrased. "What's going on in algebra that you need to avoid?" She and I had established that her means for dealing with anxiety was to avoid, and she understood that anxiety gained more and more power over her as she listened to it. She hadn't yet mastered a way to put herself in the position of power when facing down her anxiety. Sarah found ways to blame her external situations for her behaviors rather than accepting that her anxiety was choosing her behaviors for her. If she admitted that anxiety was getting in the way, she'd have to face it. She wasn't ready to do this yet.

"I hate him," she said, looking away from me. "I'm not going. I just hate him. That's why I'm not going. That's why I'll never go."

"It sounds like you're really angry at him," I reflected back to her.

"I am. He called the nurse in front of everyone and told her to come escort me to the bathroom! I'm never going back."

I cringed and empathized, "That must've been embarrassing."

"Who does that!? He didn't trust me so that's how he tried to make me stay!"

"You believe he doesn't trust you."

"He doesn't!"

"Tell me more about that."

She looked at me, annoyed, because she knew I already knew why he didn't trust her. She'd left on several occasions to go to the bathroom and had been caught in the hallway with friends or had stayed in the bathroom for thirty minutes texting friends.

Her annoyance dissipated somewhat, and she cocked her head to the side, half-smiled, and said, "I'll just do it on my own. I don't need Mr. Johnson."

"I'm hearing that you want to keep learning math." I reflected that she wanted to keep learning math in spite of being embarrassed by Mr. Johnson. I chose to focus on the fact that she still wanted to do math because this was resilience in the face of anxiety. This indicated that anxiety was getting in the way of what she wanted, and this was what I was hoping she would begin to see.

"I'm probably going to do online school anyway. I can't go back there."

"I'm curious about your word choice. Tell me more about what you mean when you say, 'You can't go back?'"

"I can't go in there if he won't let me leave," the words came tumbling out now. "I have to know that I can leave when I want to, otherwise, I can't be there. Even if he says that he'll follow the plan and let me leave when I ask, he won't let me."

Based on Sarah's history, I understood why this would be important to her. I thought about a fact her mother had shared with me: when she was little, Sarah would hide under the bed in her room and shut the lights off when her father was on a rampage. Looking at Sarah's disciplinary history, it was easy to see that confrontation always led to flight. She would literally run away and hide from teachers when they tried to assert power over her or get her to comply. I suspected that the trauma of her childhood forced Sarah into the belief that she would avoid any threatening situation, any situation with no escape route, at all costs. To her, to remain in a highly anxious state that in any way resembled the trauma of her past probably felt impossible. It made sense for her to flee rather than to face confrontation.

I continued to focus on her use of the word "can't" and asked, "When I hear you say you 'can't,' it sounds to me like you've given your anxiety a lot of power over what you can and can't do."

"I don't know, but wherever I am, I always need to know that I can get out when I start to feel panicked."

"So you need to feel safe, and if you don't, your urge is to get out."

"I guess so, and if I can't leave, I don't feel comfortable."

"How can we make sure you feel safe in Mr. Johnson's classroom so you don't need to leave?"

"He just needs to follow the plan instead of just saying he will."

I decided to challenge Sarah here: "Do you always follow the plan?"

She looked away and then spit out, "No, but that's because I get so mad at them."

"So if you're mad at the teachers, you don't have to follow your plan?"

"Well, if they wouldn't make me mad, I could follow the plan."

"If you could keep from feeling mad, you could follow your plan."

She knew where I was going with this, knew I was going to try and make her accountable in some way. She chose to dig in and resist. "I'm not going. I can't."

I thought about Sarah's insistence on the word "can't" and the fact that she'd never once spoken a word to me about her biological father. I knew about the decade of abuse Sarah had witnessed only because her mother told me. It made sense that Sarah's resistance felt inevitable and intractable to her, but it seemed like pure orneriness to just about everyone else. I decided to encourage her to imagine a perspective different than her own—that of her teachers.

"I've heard you use the word 'can't' a few times now, and that word changes how teachers view your situation," I said. "I think sometimes to adults it seems like you 'won't' go to class or follow your plan. Do you see how it might seem that you're *choosing* to defy your teachers just to make them angry?"

Sarah smirked at this and seemed to accept the theory. She liked it, I thought, because it gave her power in the situation, which starkly contrasted with her feeling of helplessness. "Once it's ruined, it's done," she snapped. "It can't be fixed."

"You mean the relationship between you and Mr. Johnson can't be fixed."

"I hate him," she said. "I'm not going back. Why can't I just stay in the hallway during his class and do my work here?"

I was connecting Sarah's apparent belief that there was no repairing the relationship between her and her teacher once it was ruptured to the relationship she had with her biological father, whom she hadn't seen since the day of the divorce. I had to help her dismantle the belief that all relationships (especially those with adult males), once strained, were beyond repair. I needed an example to gently challenge Sarah's thinking—luckily, an ideal example presented itself just a week prior.

Sarah had come to my office during her math class one day, and when I wouldn't allow her to stay, pushing her to return to class and work through her discomfort, she'd been extremely angry. She'd returned to class and finished the school day, but her mother couldn't get Sarah back to school for the following two days. When she returned, she confided that she felt betrayed by me, the person who had been her safety net when she was feeling anxious. When I called her into my office to process what had happened, she reluctantly shared that she didn't trust me anymore. "You don't believe me that my anxiety is real. You think I can sit in class and be okay, but I can't."

"You think I made you do something you couldn't do," I reflected.

"Yeah," she said, "and I had to draw the whole hour to deal, and I didn't learn any math."

I asked if the drawing helped her cope with the discomfort, establishing that she'd actually found some pretty decent coping mechanisms by enduring math class, and I challenged her by reminding her that she was, in fact, able to stay in class without anything catastrophic happening. I celebrated these successes with her, and she reluctantly took credit for beating her anxiety, even if just for that day. I took some time to talk about my role as her counselor: her cheerleader, her ally, and someone who would help her make progress in managing her anxiety even if it meant that I had to push her sometimes. I explained that pushing herself through the discomfort was the only way to decrease it. This was a crucial moment in Sarah's growth, one in which her resistance seemed to be dissolving, if even just a little bit. I'd pushed her to face her anxiety, and even though she was angry with me, we'd recovered. We'd had a break in the trust but we were able to communicate and restore our relationship because I attempted to see her experience through her lens and I'd been transparent with her about my intentions and my own feelings, which I hoped would allow her to understand my choices.

So when Sarah declared that things could never be fixed after being broken, I hoped that by gently challenging that statement, I could help her transfer what she'd experienced with me to the relationship she was developing with her teacher.

"Your relationship with Mr. Johnson is pretty strained right now," I said. "I would say you and I have been strained before, too. Did we fix things?"

She mustered, "I guess." Before I could ask how we'd managed it— because I truly wanted to know how, in her eyes, we'd been able to overcome the fractures—Sarah sputtered angrily, "But that's because you know why I do the things I do!"

Somehow Sarah felt that I understood her, and this seemed to matter to her. I asked for clarification. "Do you mean that I get why you might need to leave class?"

"Yeah," she answered. "My teachers just think I'm an asshole."

I couldn't help but laugh a little at her choice of words. She was in a better place now, less confrontational than she'd been five minutes earlier, and this time the idea of teachers thinking she was being defiant didn't produce a smirk of self-satisfaction at angering them. Instead, she'd come around to sharing her experience with me in her own words.

"How could we get teachers to understand why you do what you do?" I asked. In asking the question, I was also hoping that she would be able to look inward and articulate for herself why she was feeling so much anxiety and why she was choosing the behaviors she was choosing as a way to cope. My hope was that the shift inward would move her toward facing down her anxiety so she could keep learning math even though she felt discomfort in the classroom. Additionally, I was hoping that communication with her teacher would incite compassion from Mr. Johnson and create an opening to mend the relationship between teacher and student.

Sarah shrugged at first without saying anything, but I remained silent to let her ponder why this might be an important step. After a few moments passed, she asked, "Do you think Mr. Johnson cares?"

"I do think he cares, and I think he cares so much that he is doing whatever he can to keep you in the classroom because he knows how much you love math. And I can work with him to come up with a better way to keep you in class, one that doesn't involve calling a nurse escort to the bathroom."

She rolled her eyes and laughed, and then she sat still for a moment. Even her bouncing leg was still, as she contemplated taking this risk. And then she asked, "Will you go with me to talk to Mr. Johnson?"

I did a backflip inside and then reassured her, "Of course I will go with you."

This felt like a breakthrough moment. Reframing the experience seemed to shift Sarah's thoughts about mending the relationship, and she was able to transfer the experience of restoring a relationship to a completely new situation. Her past life experiences had taught her that communicating her vulnerabilities or communicating at all when she felt afraid was not an option available to her, but she was beginning to see it was a viable option. Sarah literally hid from those who threatened her in order to cope with anxiety; she needed to flee in order to be safe. But she was beginning to recognize that for her, intense feelings of fear were not always rational and could be endured and even appeased by facing them and sharing them with others in her world. She was willing to take some constructive action to manage her anxiety rather than avoid it at all costs, and this felt like immense progress to me.

Although this was an important step in Sarah's progress, it was just the start of some semblance of self-realization. She was beginning to understand how she existed in the world, and she was starting to make positive changes. Sarah was asking herself important questions, and she seemed open to looking for answers, which she hoped to find as she was now willing to work with a psychologist outside of school. Rather than avoiding her anxiety and denying that anxiety had a hold on her, she was ready to face it by reaching out for help, which was perhaps the single most important step in her growth.

The remainder of the year continued with ups and downs in which Sarah retreated into avoidance but she rebounded much more quickly. Her developing self-awareness and ability to use tools to remain calm even when anxiety threatened allowed her to remain in most of her classes; remarkably, after her conversation with Mr. Johnson, she never had to leave algebra class again. Fortunately, Mr. Johnson was warm and empathic during our meeting, and he modeled taking ownership of mistakes by acknowledging his own missteps. Sarah told Mr. Johnson about her anxiety and what made her feel safe, and they were able to create a plan that allowed Sarah to feel safe and Mr. Johnson to feel respected. Notably, the self-talk she designed for herself to remain in algebra included the following: "I'm safe in this classroom because Mr. Johnson gets me."

Two weeks left in the school year, Sarah made an appointment to see me. She told the counseling secretary, "No, it's not an emergency." She said she'd just like to catch up before the school year was over. She was wearing a new pair of Vans slip-ons, and she was dressed sharply in leggings and a sporty hoodie. She had brought a notebook, opened to her four-year plan for high school—one page in its entirety, neatly penned, but without the complexity of her sixth-grade planner—and she was beaming about the prospect of a future where she is authentically herself and freed from the grip of her anxiety and her traumatic past.

CASE DISCUSSION

As one might suspect, resistance is not uncommon when working with middle school students, and Sarah, who so clearly needed help navigating her world, provided me with a lively introduction to working with resistance in school counseling. When I first met Sarah as a sixth grader, she seemed to ward off my attempts to understand her by maintaining straight A's and nodding politely, if uncomfortably, when we met briefly each week. My attempts to connect with her seemed to miss the mark, and I began to question myself—if I couldn't connect with this kid sitting in front of me, how would I help her? As I look back, I now see that we *were* forging ahead with a relationship, but because it was on Sarah's terms, I initially missed this. When I learned that she was diagnosed with generalized anxiety disorder and her 504 indicated we were to learn and practice calming strategies, I was ready to delve in. I was comfortable talking about Sarah's anxiety and how to manage it, but she resisted my attempts to discuss how she experienced her world. I wanted to hear about her goals, her dreams, and most importantly (in my mind), her fears so that we could move past them; I wanted to "fix her" so her anxiety wouldn't get in the way of her academic, social, and emotional success. But Sarah wasn't going there with me, and since she was getting straight A's and I'd heard no concerns from teachers, I assumed that she was managing just fine and didn't press her.

We bobbed along, slowly getting to know one another, and it wasn't until Sarah's eighth grade year that I realized these weekly meetings and the comfort they offered her became a safety net for Sarah when her anxiety became too much to bear. I realize that meeting with a student weekly isn't a norm in school counseling, but fortunately in this instance, her 504 plan indicated the meetings.

When in eighth grade, Sarah began to lash out at me and her teachers and became defiant in an attempt to avoid situations that caused her distress. Initially I was surprised by the changes I saw in her behavior. But when I considered her life experience and her way of coping until that point, it made more sense to me. Sarah's new way of managing her anxiety was just as effective as getting straight A's and maintaining a perfect image, if more desperate. She had quickly mastered the art of cutting remarks, and teachers, despite trying to establish a positive relationship with Sarah, began to throw up their hands or ask for more severe consequences for her escalating behaviors. And although Sarah's resistance to explore her inner world with me never completely dissolved, she seemed to trust me more after she discovered I wouldn't judge her or dismiss her feelings when she was authentic with me.

There seemed to be three angles to Sarah's resistance. Freud (1917) believed that resistance in therapy served to protect clients from extreme emotional pain, but he also asserted that resistance was an indication that the client was moving closer to addressing buried emotional pain. Freud's explanation of resistance may explain why Sarah deflected attempts to discuss her feelings of anxiety. For example, when I asked Sarah how her body felt when she was anxious in an attempt to help her identify signals that she may need to use her calming strategies, she responded repeatedly, saying, "I don't know." When I pushed, she abruptly got up and while walking out the door said, "I'm good! I have all A's." I wondered if Sarah felt threatened that I would begin a full-scale exploration of her family dynamic when we talked about anxiety.

Sarah's resistance may also have served to protect her from others who were claiming to help her, like her father and her mother, who had abandoned her physically and emotionally. Her caregivers were inconsistent and untrustworthy, so she may have deduced that I would be the same. In this way, Sarah's resistance provided some stability in the foreign and unstable new environment of middle school. Her highly fractured and violent early childhood seemed to make her skeptical of anyone who was trying to establish a relationship with her and quick to quit a relationship. As she stated in the incident detailed earlier, "Once it's ruined, it's done." I respected her need to wear her figurative armor so as not to become vulnerable in an unknown setting with an unknown person. This respect for her boundaries and my patience made pushing through some of Sarah's resistance possible later on. Sarah's resistance also seemed to serve the purpose of protecting her perfect self-image, and Sarah attempted to protect this self-concept at a high cost. Letting go of this perfect ideal would be losing too much.

Cognitive therapists look at resistance as a way to protect a client from too much change or disruption of the client's reality (Mahoney, 1988). For Sarah, if she acknowledged that her life, specifically her family life and her inner life, was in disarray, she would have to abandon her belief that she could structure her school life prescriptively enough to ward off any chaos or unexpected bumps. I saw Sarah's monumental attempts to keep a stranglehold on her academic life when I'd glimpsed that tiny, artistic "lights out" entry in her planner. I realized then that there was no room for vulnerability or loss of control in that day, and I was glad for the time we'd spent establishing a solid relationship. This elaborate planner was evidence of her attempt to resist disruption of this carefully constructed reality. Her anxiety caused her to clutch at control of her life until it became too much for her. I tried to offer her coping mechanisms for her anxiety and ways to self-soothe when I sensed she was feeling overwhelmed, but she dismissed deep breathing and self-talk as "weird" and acted as if she didn't need the tools, unwilling to share her inner struggle with anxiety even though it was evident outwardly. And when defiant behaviors began to surface, she shifted the blame outward and refused to accept responsibility and refused to look inward at why she may have behaved in a certain way.

As an eleven-year-old, Sarah was amid major developmental changes and on the cusp of moving from concrete to formal operational thinking. Over the course of the three years I worked with Sarah, I was aware of how stuck she seemed to be in concrete thinking. Hypothesizing and contemplating cause-and-effect relationships was almost impossible for Sarah. She was unable to link her feelings, behaviors, and situations. Schave and Schave (1989) call this the "time warp" concept: if young adolescents were able to link these events, they might be overwhelmed by guilt, shame, or anger; the time warp allows them to avoid responsibility. Sarah was a master at this, and I found that her limitations in formal operational thinking made some of the CBT work I was trying to do with her difficult.

Whereas many middle school students are able to see future possibilities based on their behaviors, Sarah was not able to link her behaviors to events that took place in her life. Initially, when Sarah refused to own her part in a problematic situation, I suspected she was intentionally avoiding the conversation to evade a consequence. But as our work together continued, I realized that she seemed to be, for the most part, incapable of making "in-the-moment" decisions based on the results of her decisions. Sarah was unable to entertain the idea of "either-or" and made poor decisions since she couldn't generate alternatives to cope with her anxiety and anger. When she was cursing at teachers or skipping class, she was incapable of making decisions based on the future outcomes; her brain was hijacked by anxiety, and therefore her decisions were based on self-preservation rather than the outcome.

And when I tried to process these behaviors with Sarah, she denied that the version of the story I received from the teacher was accurate. In fact, she often denied she even spoke to the reporting teacher, even when video cameras proved she had not only spoken to the teacher, but also had gesticulated aggressively with both middle fingers, thrown her books to the floor, and then stormed off to the bathroom. I found her denial extremely frustrating and wondered how it came to be that she was incapable of owning her part in any problematic behaviors. It was as if she could not bring herself to admit she had made an error. If she did, her perfectly constructed self-image would be shattered, but if she denied the event took place, she could hold onto the idea that she was not flawed. In those moments of vulnerability when I provided empathy and acknowledged her feelings of sadness and fear, I believe Sarah began to trust me. With a humanistic approach, I was able to connect with Sarah, build our relationship, and have some healthy confrontations. More importantly, she was able to transfer behaviors learned with me to her relationships with teachers.

Early in my career as school counselor, Sarah's resistance felt insurmountable, but her case continues to provide me with a reminder to trust in the therapeutic relationship when working with young adolescents who are undergoing immense changes in development and, in addition, are coping with many adverse childhood experiences. Sarah's case presented layers and layers of psychological material and various therapeutic approaches to consider, but the therapeutic alliance seemed to provide the foundation for psychological healing.

I feel compelled to share that my in-depth case conceptualization of Sarah was born purely out of an attempt to discover how to help students like Sarah to succeed and thrive in school. I began writing this case study to help me understand my students who struggle with anxiety. I hoped that through writing, I could unearth some answers, especially when students were not receiving psychological support outside of school.

When cases like Sarah's present themselves, we can rely on our training in theory to guide our decisions and conceptualize a case in order to understand our student's reality. We can use our knowledge of theory to inform our practice and to recognize why a student may be behaving in a certain way. Sarah presents a case in which the student needed more psychological help than a school counselor could provide, but my understanding of theory helped me to understand why she was choosing certain behaviors and allowed me to approach her situation with awareness and compassion. Much of my thinking on the topic of Sarah was done on my drive home and while lying in bed at night rather than at school; generally, there is no time for an in-depth case conceptualization in the school setting, but I found my education in theory crucial as I worked with Sarah. I also want to note that fostering relationships between teachers and students is one of the most powerful tools we have in helping our students succeed and helping our school cultures to thrive, and in this instance, it was transformative. I'm lucky to work with a group of compassionate teachers who do everything they can to meet the needs of all students.

DISCUSSION QUESTIONS

1. What are some strategies to utilize while helping Sarah build her relationship with Mr. Johnson?
2. How could a student's history of trauma impact your decisions when using humanistic counseling?
3. As a school counselor, what American School Counseling Association national model standards are you addressing? Are there any ethical codes to be concerned about?
4. What would you share with the high school counseling staff when Sarah transitions to high school?
5. If you don't have the opportunity to meet weekly or even yearly with each of your students, what are ways that you can foster relationships with your students?
6. Is Sarah a student who could benefit from special education services? How would this type of support benefit her? If you feel that special education is not appropriate, explain why.

REFERENCES

Freud, S. (1917). Introductory lectures on psycho-analysis. *The standard edition of the complete psychological works of Sigmund Freud* (Vol. 15). London: Hogarth Press and the Institute of Psycho-Analysis.

Mahoney, M. J. (1988). Constructive metatheory: Implications for psychotherapy. *International Journal of Personal Construct Psychology, 1*, 299–316.

Rogers, C. R. (1951). *Client-centered therapy.* Oxford: Houghton Mifflin.

Schave, D., & Schave, B. F. (1989). *Early adolescence and the search for self: A developmental perspective.* New York: Praeger.

Chapter Three

Alicia, Sarah, Angie, and James

The task of being a school counselor in America today looks drastically different than it did fifty years ago. What began as a position to help students prepare for vocational and career development in the 1950s has now expanded to support the whole student within the counseling domains of career readiness, academics, and social/emotional well-being. Passing handwritten notes is a thing of the past; now students use the internet and social media to communicate with their peers. Phones provide students with access to infinite amounts of information and they can share infinite amounts of information in a split second; the entire world is quite literally in the palms of their hands.

In this rapidly changing school environment, it is imperative that school counselors hold on to Carl Rogers's teachings of unconditional positive regard for all students; even when the world appears vastly different from the one in which we grew up, we must trust our belief in the innate goodness of children as the anchor for our work with students as they navigate growing up in a fast-paced and dynamic world. The following case study discusses the way that social media ignited a racially charged event and how Carl Rogers's core belief, in addition to culturally competent counseling strategies, guided me in this situation (Rogers, 1951).

My attempts to provide a comfortable, supportive, and affirming environment for all of my students lay at the core of my practice. In order to do this, I have spent time exploring my own unconscious biases based on my beliefs and upbringing. Students come to me to share moments when they have felt uncomfortable as a result of racial inequity. Students of color have reported to me that a teacher allowed a white student to go to the bathroom but refused a minute later when an African American student asked to go. Students of color have also reported feeling targeted for dress code violations, and they also have shared that teachers don't encourage them to do honors courses whereas white students with similar grades are urged to enroll in these classes. In order to fully have positive regard for students, counselors must remain honest about their current blind spots and their need for cross-cultural growth. I hope this case study encourages all counselors to look inward to identify potential growth areas because our students deserve this from us.

As you read this case study, look for the following:

- How the counselor addresses his own implicit bias to meet the needs of his students.
- How the counselor uses culturally competent counseling strategies in his practice.
- How could the counselor promote a healthy and culturally responsive school climate?

CASE STUDY INTRODUCTION

I work at a high school located about twenty minutes outside Minneapolis. This school is a unique blend of students living in various parts of the metro area. Historically, the school has been predominantly white, especially among the staff. The current demographic is roughly 60 percent white, 18 percent African American, 13 percent Asian, and 5 percent Hispanic. I have the opportunity to work with students who span the socioeconomic spectrum, one minute meeting with the owner of a new BMW, and the next, with a student whose family is homeless. The school embraces the collection of students and prides itself on being family. In the following case study, this point of pride is tested to the utmost.

INCIDENT

The volleyball team wrapped up the regular season with a 10–2 record, qualifying for the state tournament, and on the bus ride home, spirits were high and the team was playing Big Sean's, "Blessed." What took place on this bus ride would change the tone of the entire school year.

A white student sang along, while her white friend recorded her and posted the video on Instagram.

> Funny thing about talkin' behind my back
> Is that it just keep comin' back to me nigga
> Was all for a sec now it's back to me nigga.

Immediately, one student of color posted online saying, "Wow this is so messed up!" Another posted, "Take this down, look at this!?!" The video spread on social media, negative feedback streamed in, and soon the local news picked up the story.

The game was on a Tuesday, and by Thursday, the climate in the high school was toxic, the student body divided. On one side of the issue was students who empathized with the two white students; these folks argued that the intent wasn't to offend, rather the girls were just having fun. On the other side, many people felt the incident required a response that included mediation, restorative justice, and education surrounding race relations. The girls did not receive a consequence from the school for their actions.

Adding to the tension in the building, racial slurs stating, "I hate black people," appeared in three bathroom stalls, and offensive remarks popped up on social media: "We brought you here. Without us you wouldn't be anything." Students of color shared their rage, heartbreak, fear, and betrayal with me, and I felt these emotions with them. Students of color reported their dismay that the girls hadn't received a consequence, and they shared their disillusionment as they watched what they perceived to be injustice. One of my African American students observed, "These girls are the best female athletes in the building; they're white and teachers adore them. They are very protected."

Many students, especially students of color, were not surprised that the students didn't receive a consequence. They shared that microaggressions had been happening to them frequently up until this point with no consequences. I began to hear more and more expressions of anger from students of color.

In an attempt to channel the anger and to be heard, students both African American and Caucasian at the high school organized a peaceful protest and walkout that was attended by more than two hundred students. The students' stated purpose was to raise awareness about racism and discrimination at the school; they wanted to be heard and proposed more education and open dialogue about race relations at the high school and in the community. As students headed toward the main entrance, some were carrying signs that said, "No justice, no peace," or "Ignorance needs education." Many students protested by sitting quietly in the school's main entryway, and as the space began to fill up, many began to stand around the outside. At times students chanted, "No justice, no peace." Throughout the morning, students periodically took the floor to present their demands of the school's staff. They asked for a "conversation about race and equity," and they persisted for the better part of the morning. By noon, the students had disassembled and returned to class.

Supporting high school students during this event that caused such upheaval within the student body was a roller coaster for me as a counselor.

Throughout the week we had to manage the range of emotions and reactions from students and staff and also to attend to my own emotions. This ended up being one of the toughest moments of my career as a school counselor. As one of two African American licensed staff in the building, it was tough to hear other staff discount the feelings and emotions of our students of color, and it was uncomfortable when coworkers would stop talking about the situation going on at school whenever I approached. When parents who didn't know I was African American called in to discuss their anger about how African American students were creating disruption at the school and suggested that they were considering transferring their students to another district where "this type of behavior isn't tolerated," I found myself feeling defensive and angry in response. Crafting my words in response to these comments challenged me on many levels.

Two African American girls, Alicia and Sara, both juniors, came into my office, and I was glad for the previous conversations I'd had with both of them about college aspirations because we'd already developed a positive relationship. The girls came to the counseling office on the morning of the planned protest, and I could see that they were agitated. Alicia was taking measured quick breaths, fists clenching and unclenching, and Sara stomped her foot and ground her shoe into the carpet as if she were killing a bug. Alicia asked, "Mr. Francis, did you hear what's going on at noon?"

I played dumb, pretending like I didn't know about the planned protest: "Yeah, I hear we have class." They exchanged a glance between themselves, and Sara retorted, "That's when the protest starts today. Did you hear about what is going on?"

I responded, "Yes, I heard about the protest," then asked the girls, "Do you think a lot of students will go?"

Sara replied, "We've been organizing the students on social media, and I think lots of kids are coming. We're bringing a peaceful message, but it's a strong message. We just want to be heard. We're tired of stuff like this happening at our school and no one doing anything about it. The teachers and principals don't believe us when we tell them how we feel." So many memories came to mind in this moment. I could relate to the students because I remembered my own experience as an African American student in high school. I, too, had moments in high school in which I was treated poorly but didn't speak up, so I found myself admiring their courage. The girls were excited to speak their minds, to have their voices heard, to stand up for themselves, and they were full of hope that their actions could create change. Although they were excited about instigating change, they also were concerned about the reaction from teachers and staff and worried that they'd be viewed as troublemakers. I wondered what my role here should be. I contemplated helping them form a powerful and persuasive message, and I wanted to walk them through possible outcomes, but I refrained. I suggested that they stay positive and peaceful and that they should expect that some students and staff may get uncomfortable. I also encouraged the girls to share how the situation made them feel when they spoke during the protest.

Alicia expressed that the tension had been palpable in the classrooms and stated, "It has been hard to focus in class because I know the situation is on everyone's mind but no one is talking about it. Seems like no one wants to bring it up." At one point in the conversation, Alicia paused to ask me, "You are with us, aren't you?"

Part of me wanted to exclaim, "Hell, yeah, I'm with y'all!" but instead I said, "I fully support you, and I'll be with you on the sidelines. This is your chance to speak out, and this is your moment, not mine. I'm proud of you for taking a stand." As I pledged my support to Alicia and Sara, I was mindful of the many staff who dismissed the protesting students' feelings.

Relying on a humanistic approach to guide my decisions, I began by establishing congruence. I needed the students to know that I am human, African American, and a real person who could relate to their feelings. I let Alicia and Sara know that I was with them and could empathize with how they felt. I wanted to make sure Alicia and Sara felt heard, had a space to talk openly about race, and knew that an adult at the school supported them, free from judgment. I found it especially important to validate Alicia and Sara's feelings around their experience. I shared that I also get tired of encountering situations of discrimination and could understand their concern regarding not being heard. I expressed, "What you two are feeling right now is real, and I get that it hurts. I know it gets tiring to have to think about these kinds of situations every day when you come to school and those feelings build up. I feel it, too." One of the girls then shared, "I get tired of being one of the few black students in classes, and when I share how I am feeling, it sometimes feels like people here don't believe this is going on. Do you see it, Mr. Francis?"

"I experience it, too. If you think it is hard being a student here, imagine being one of maybe seven educators of color in the building. I see it every day, too. And when I see it, I try and fix it. I'm wired to be compassionate and forgiving, and I think it's helped me to get through some of those tough experiences." I tried to align myself with the girls while still instilling hope that their actions could instigate change.

About an hour into the protest, one of the school security staff asked me to connect with a student that he found crying in the hall. Her name was Angie, a ninth grader, and I had worked with her previously to help her change her schedule. Angie, face red and wet with tears, was still choking back sobs as she entered my office. Her dark hair was in a ponytail, and she wore a hoodie and baggy, torn jeans. I shepherded Angie into my office and allowed her to collect herself. After about five minutes she began to explain why she was crying: "I don't get why they are mad at me for not going down there. I don't think it's right. I don't support that kinda stuff, and they know I don't want to, but they won't leave me alone about not going." Angie continued to cry while she spoke, and she went on, "I just made friends, like two months ago, and I don't want to lose them, but I just don't feel right about going to the protest."

I responded, "I imagine that has to be hard to feel pressure from friends you are just getting to know." Angie continued to cry. I continued, "I can tell you are feeling sad and hurt. It can be hard getting to know new people at times." I wondered what she meant by stating that she "didn't feel right about going to the protest." Did she feel that because she was white, she shouldn't go?

I found it very important at this moment to use unconditional positive regard. It was not appropriate for me to share my opinion with Angie or to disregard her current feelings. I was also mindful that Angie may have felt uncomfortable sharing her reluctance to protest because I am African American, and the purpose of the protest was to raise awareness of and put a stop to racial prejudice within the school. During my conversation with Angie, her mother called, and I spoke to her for the first time. Angie's mother started the conversation by asking, "Is Angie in there with you?" When I told her that she was in my office, she continued, "Good, I hear you all have a bunch of students causing a disruption in school and protesting. Some of her friends wanted her to go." I let her mom know that I was aware of the protest. Her mother continued, "I am glad she didn't go down there. She does not need to be down there around that trouble. I can't believe you guys are allowing this to happen at school. Not a good way to start the year. I thought it was a good school." I shared with Angie's mother that some students at school felt hurt by things that happened recently and decided to share their opinions. Her mother was abrupt at this point, cutting the conversation short, and expressed again that she "was just glad Angie didn't get involved in that mess." After my conversation with Angie's mom, I felt I'd gained some insight into Angie's experience. Angie was looking for someone to validate her feelings of isolation; for her, this moment was about feeling excluded, not about racism, and it was my job to recognize this. I validated Angie's feelings about being left out and misunderstood and reminded her that "Even for adults, emotion-laden topics like racism are extremely difficult to talk about with friends."

The day continued with students and staff stopping into the counseling office to offer their reactions to the students' peaceful protest. The organized protest included students sitting silently, interrupted by a few speeches requesting conversations about race and demanding social justice. Some students carried signs and some chanted for "hope" and "change." The protest started inside the building and then flowed outside in front of the school. Some teachers completely ignored the protest and discouraged students from attending. One teacher even said that students participating in the protest should be arrested. Some of the teachers facilitated discussions about the incident that took place on the volleyball team's bus, and in these classrooms, students shared their feelings about race relations in their school.

Throughout the day, teachers shared details of classroom discussions and staff shared differing viewpoints and perspectives regarding the incident. Although staff tried to be respectful in their discourse, tension gripped the school, and when the final bell rang, I felt myself breathe a sigh of relief. Soon after the bell, James, a white twelfth grader, ducked into my office and grabbed a seat. My relationship with James was unique because we realized early on that we had many similarities. James was a middle child, extroverted, loved music concerts, and had a job at a restaurant, and over the course of our weekly check-ins, we'd developed a strong relationship. James usually checked in during first period because he had a TV journalism class, which allowed him to walk around and interview people.

James asked, "Mr. Francis, how are you doing with everything that happened today?" Initially, I was struck by James's genuine concern. I wondered if I should give him a polished, professional school counselor response or if I should take a risk and be transparent. I said, "Actually, James, this is probably one of the most frustrating days I've had as a school counselor."

James asked, "Have you experienced racism, like when you were in high school?"

"Yes, and I guess today just reminded me that we still have a long way to go."

James continued, "Yeah, I guess I agree. And I feel confused about it all. Like I don't really get how African American people use the 'N' word, and it's in a ton of popular songs, but African Americans are offended when white people use the word."

Prior to the conversation with James, I had talked about race in great depth with other students, usually African American students. Our conversations usually revolved around the shared experience of racism and understanding the dual-consciousness of being African American in a predominately white setting. With the relationship that I had established with James over the years, we both felt comfortable having an authentic talk about race. Prior to this, I had assumed that white students would not be interested in or feel uncomfortable hearing about my experience as a black male and educator. This was a landmark moment in my counseling career. I made the assumption that white students wouldn't be interested in hearing my story because I had never been asked to share my perspective or experience with racism as a student nor as an educator—such conversations were not had. But today was different.

James and I, because of our solid relationship, were able to forge ahead and talk about our different perspectives. I shared my perspective, as an

African American male, on the use of the "N" word by white people. I began, "I can only share my personal feelings about this topic, but for me, if a black friend of mine used the 'N' word with me, I wouldn't be upset, but if a white person said it to me, I would be offended. And here's why." I took a minute to explain the history of the word and shared how the use of the word by a white person brought about a history of violent oppression that was just simply too much to swallow. I shared that the "N" word carried too much weight to be tossed about without considering how its use makes another human feel. I said, "When another African American person uses that word with me, it doesn't imply power over me." James nodded his head in response to my explanation, and he simply said, "I get it." I don't know if he really understood the depth of my meaning, but his acknowledgment felt huge in the moment. It gave me hope after a long day in which human compassion and connection were missing, and I reflected on the fact the human relationships lie at the core of our work as school counselors. It's the way to bridge chasms, and it's essential to instigating change.

It often feels like the school climate doesn't foster authentic conversations about race and culture. I understand the many reasons why staff, students, parents, and the school community avoid these conversations, although I wish we felt safer to be open to discussions that could promote growth in the area of cultural competence. I have witnessed the discomfort in my white colleagues' faces when the topic of racism comes up in my presence. White people tend to avoid conversations with me about race in predominantly white spaces. Perhaps people feel guilty, incompetent, or afraid that they might offend me. I find myself worried about making others uncomfortable when I share my authentic opinions or experiences. Interestingly, when I worked in a predominately African American school, conversations about race and racism were prevalent. Before taking a group of African American students on a college visit, I stated without even a thought, "I want you all to think about stereotypes before we set foot on campus. Let's present an image that defies all negative and racist stereotypes. Let's represent our school with your best." I found it comfortable speaking with my students about race because I was African American, just like them, and in a predominantly white setting, I felt unsure about how to approach the topic of racism with students and staff.

This conversation with James was new and welcome territory; he and I could engage in authentic dialogue about a difficult topic because we had already established a solid relationship. We had built a level of trust in which we could take a leap into hard conversations and offer each other grace. Reciprocal trust and vulnerability are paramount in the counseling relationship, especially in cross-cultural settings. Whether spoken or not, in the cross-cultural counseling relationship, there are times in which the student or counselor are curious around the other's background, and doing the work to build relationships with students helps these conversations become more fluid. After this conversation with James three things happened. First, our relationship became extremely strong (I visited James and his family during campus moving-in day at my alma mater). Conversations around race with white students became an opportunity to open myself to students to explore questions they have had and to think of ways to improve our school racial climate. Third, I began sharing my story about James with other counselors and teachers and offered suggestions on ways to make discussions about race feel more comfortable by establishing trust and assuming positive intent from both parties (Sue & Sue, 2008).

CASE DISCUSSION

Culturally competent counseling practices based in humanist theory guided me through this day. Managing a situation of this magnitude in a high school left me with several revelations I believe counselors need to be mindful of in order to effectively carry out humanistic counseling and to support all students. If counselors are attempting to provide unconditional positive regard in earnest, they must be honest with themselves regarding personal biases they hold. In order to effectively support Angie, I needed to make sure I had addressed my own biases about people who did not share my perspectives about race. I attempted to address my biases in a variety of ways, and I stumbled several times through this process (Sue & Sue, 2008).

I have made incorrect assumptions during my career. Owning my mistakes and allowing my students to see me as vulnerable and fallible was the way I attempted to remedy my blunders. During my first year as a counselor, an Asian student expressed to me that he needed help with math. I listened to his worries and reassured him that with more effort and a positive outlook, he could be successful in math. Although I didn't consciously jump to the conclusion that he was good at math simply because of a stereotype, I wonder if this stereotype caused me to downplay this student's distress about his struggles with math. I wonder if I had disregarded this student's feelings. When he returned to my office, still struggling in his math class, I tried to audit myself and listen with a new awareness that I may have been making assumptions due to a stereotype.

I try and look closely at feelings of discomfort that arise and consider where my feelings are coming from and why they're emerging. I believe this constant self-monitoring is a continual process. We all have blind spots, and as I work to identify my own, I feel more compassionate and more caring as a counselor. I no longer take comfort in connecting with students who are just like me. I intentionally work to connect with students who are completely different from me, and I work to gain insights into their experiences and perspectives. I work to fill in those blind spots. For example, when I started working as a counselor, I noticed that I jumped to conclusions about students who drove certain cars. I began to question myself, "Why am I assuming that because this kid drives a BMW that he has everything handed to him?" Because I didn't drive a BMW when I was sixteen, I made assumptions, and I quickly realized that I needed to audit my assumptions. My automatic thoughts were getting in the way of authentic connections with kids, and by pressing pause on these assumptions, I was able to dismantle barriers to meaningful human relationships (Corey & Corey, 2011).

As I processed my own experiences of being an African American in a predominantly white setting, I recalled staff meetings where the room fell silent when a discussion of race emerged. I always wondered if the silence was a result of my presence. And several times, when a conversation about race continued, I was asked, "Derek, what's your take on this?" because I was the only African American in the room. Sometimes I feel disheartened knowing that many of my colleagues have not had meaningful conversations about race because they simply haven't had opportunities to work with colleagues or students of color, and this is always a reminder of how far we have to go in terms of developing our proficiency in cultural competency. I often hesitate to share my viewpoints because I worry that my experience might be dismissed or cause my colleagues to feel defensive; and if I am hesitant to share with people I respect and consider friends, I know our students are scared to bring up issues of race. But I push through my discomfort and share because I really hope that by hearing my experience, educators will be encouraged to push through their own blind spots in order to authentically connect with all of our students (Corey & Corey, 2011).

Sometimes I feel exhaustion as I try to live with one foot in both worlds, the predominantly white culture of the school setting and my African American culture, but I find that I welcome the burden of sharing the African American experience with my colleagues because I know it moves the conversation and changes mind-sets. I'm outspoken—this comes naturally to me—and I feel that my ability to discuss uncomfortable topics with compassion is something I can share with my staff. Even when the constant duplicity of maintaining cultural norms in a predominantly white environment and honoring my African American cultural norms felt like a tightrope act, I see the value.

However, experiencing the unconscious microaggressions from my white peers weighs on me. I noticed that oftentimes white staff report African American students for dress code violations when white students sitting right next to the students of color are guilty of the same offense. When I try to broach the subject, I am met with defensiveness, and this feels heavy. My duty to stand up and give voice to my black and brown students' concerns weighs on me. The times I bite my tongue because I wonder if it's worth it to say anything and the times I feel disillusioned about the future of race relations weigh on me. These experiences weigh on me, but at the same time they compel me to incite positive changes in how we get along as a racially diverse school community.

When I reflect on my own experience with race, I am made aware of what I still have to learn. Students are harmed when educators do not work through their unconscious biases. It is very important to listen to students and not discount their feelings even when we cannot fully understand their experience. A deeper awareness of our current blind spots helps school counselors provide a more welcoming, unconditional, and person-centered relationship in our always changing educational setting (Corey & Corey, 2011).

As a counselor, I do my best to listen carefully and curiously in order to understand the individual student's experience, and I express my respect for my student's unique voice and perspective. I remind students that I have not experienced what they are sharing but that I am hearing that this is how they feel. "I can see that this situation is causing you stress, and I am here with you and I want to try and understand." And as a counselor, I try and advocate for equity and social justice whenever possible. In the last year, we started social justice groups in order to help educators in our building, through year-long professional development, gain knowledge about unjust practices in the school and strategies to better serve students of all backgrounds. Part of the professional development is understanding the unconscious biases we all have, where they came from, and how to work through them. It can be difficult as an adult realizing that you have lived a good portion of your life treating certain groups of students in certain ways without being cognizant of it. The professional development time is also used as a safe space for people to share situations they have had with students or other staff and to explore ways to address these situations. The next part of the social justice professional development is to provide real-life scenarios in which staff experience a situation in which they are not in the racial majority. All of these endeavors, we hope, move us forward and allow us to disassemble our own biases in order to break down the barriers between staff and students. Since we know that relationship fosters healing and promotes individual success in our students, we owe it to our kids to do all we can to be open to establishing connections with each and every one of our unique students.

DISCUSSION QUESTIONS

1. When counselors see unconscious microaggressions occur, how should they intervene in order to promote change and self-awareness among their colleagues?

2. How do we support students when they want to exercise their right to protest against something that is occurring within our school system?
3. How do we promote explicit instruction in the area of cultural competency when it isn't welcomed?
4. How does the counselor grow in the area of cultural competency during the course of events that occurs within this case study?

REFERENCES

Corey, M., & Corey, G. (2011). *Becoming a helper.* Belmont, CA: Brooks/Cole Cengage Learning.
Rogers, C. R. (1951). *Client-centered therapy.* Oxford, England: Houghton Mifflin.
Sue, D., & Sue, D. (2008). *Counseling the Culturally Diverse.* Hoboken, NJ: John Wiley.

Part II

Adlerian Theory

The educator must believe in the potential power of his pupil, and he must employ all his art in seeking to bring his pupil to experience this power.
—Alfred Adler

Adlerian theory was chosen for part II of this book because the theory itself is embedded in the work of school counselors. One of the basic assumptions of the theory is that all individual behavior occurs in a social context. Similarly, school counselors view their students holistically through the three American School Counselor Association (ASCA) domains: emotional/social, academic, and career. Adlerian therapists encourage individuals to activate their social interests and develop new lifestyles through relationship, analysis, and action methods. Similarly, school counselors strive to help their students explore their strengths, support systems, and the control that they have over their actions. With Adlerian counseling, school counselors utilize action-oriented interventions, such as role play, the magic question, and other interactive mediations. School counselors utilize Adlerian therapy because it is fast paced, holistic, and focuses on how to move their students forward in all aspects of their lives.

The next three chapters explore how this strength-based approach is utilized at each level. Some aspects of the theory, such as birth order, are explored more freely at the high school level than at the elementary level. Each counselor utilizes Adlerian theory not only in practice, but also to explore his or her own emotional responses when working with students. Each counselor builds a working alliance with his/her student; however, notice how each counselor uses a different approach to reach that particular student. Finally, chapter 6 challenges you, the reader, to incorporate a multicultural counseling approach in addition to Adlerian counseling. Both approaches encourage exploring the student's behavior in a social context to better understand the student's social culture and world.

Chapter Four

Lawrence

At the time of this case study, I was working at two elementary schools in the U.S. Midwest. The school district in which this case study took place served a diverse population, including African American, Asian, Hispanic, American Indian, and white students. Many students received English language services, and many also qualified for free or reduced lunches. The school district comprised areas that were home to many immigrant families who spoke languages other than English at home.

As you read this case study, look for the following:

- How the school counselor used Adlerian theory to understand the student's behavior and to select strategies to help the student succeed.
- Using the student's interests and strengths as a basis for the school counselor and the student's work together.
- The school counselor's awareness of her own emotional responses to the student and the ways that she handled these self-observations.
- The importance of classroom lessons in the school counselor's comprehensive school counseling program.

CASE STUDY INTRODUCTION

Lawrence, an African American male kindergartener, was one of the younger kindergarteners that school year, having just turned five years old two months prior to the start of school. He attended a racially diverse elementary school where most students qualified for free or reduced lunches. During the previous two years, the principal had made social-emotional learning a clear priority to all staff at the school in an effort to get students' behaviors better under control and to create a more peaceful learning community.

47

INCIDENT

I first met Lawrence in my school counselor classroom lessons at the beginning of the school year. I met with the principal just after the start of the school year to discuss which students we anticipated might have the greatest social-emotional needs and how I could help. We agreed that a large part of my role that year was to support the kindergarteners' social-emotional development. Most kindergarteners had not attended preschool, and many had just moved to the United States and had no experience with American school. Compared to the many students with high social-emotional needs, Lawrence did not initially stand out. In fact, I hardly remembered him during the first few weeks. He was quiet and followed directions without complaint. I quickly learned he was one of the few students who could be trusted to complete activities independently and happily. He had the biggest, most infectious smile. His bright eyes combined with his attentive, curious demeanor gave the immediate impression that this was a student who was quickly and eagerly taking in the new world around him. There were many other students with behavioral and social-emotional struggles who took much of my attention. Of all the students in the class, I did not expect Lawrence to develop behavioral or social-emotional concerns. So I was very surprised when, around December, it appeared that he became an entirely different person.

All of a sudden, it seemed, his behavior in class completely changed. He would be a model student one moment, and would become completely dysregulated the next. He would not follow directions. He would throw blocks at other students. He would run around the classroom, climb the bookshelves, and jump off. Though his behavior was different than what I had seen in September, his demeanor had not changed: he was still joyful, bright, and shining, but now he delighted in disrupting. Class seemed to be a game to him, and he won by thoroughly disrupting his classroom and my school counselor lessons. And no redirection, time-out, or extra work consequence seemed to make any difference. I was at a loss as to the reason for this change in Lawrence's behavior, but knew I needed to figure out some strategies as soon as possible—both for his long-term success in school and to preserve a positive learning environment in the classroom for the sake of the other students.

I considered my observations of Lawrence through an Adlerian lens. In particular, I thought a lot about the goals of Lawrence's behavior. Adler emphasized that all children's behavior is goal driven, even though children likely are not aware of the goals of their behavior (Dreikurs, 1964). Ultimately, children desire belonging and contributing to their social communities (Dreikurs, 1964). I considered Adler's four "mistaken goals" of misbehavior, in particular that of "power seeking" (Sweeney, 1989, p. 154). When I reflected that one of the characteristics of the power seeking is that a child's behavior intensifies when redirected (Positive Discipline, 2018), I knew I was on to something. One of the most challenging aspects of Lawrence's behavior was that no redirection seemed to help; in fact, redirection tended to escalate his behavior. It was all part of his game. Once I decided I would move forward with the hypothesis that Lawrence's behavior was directed by the misguided power goal, I considered what strategies or skills might help Lawrence meet his need for power in a positive, productive way. I wanted to help him develop genuine relationships with adults and peers around him and contribute to a school community where he could fill his keen mind with all the knowledge of the world that he would need in his life.

I called Lawrence's mother to learn about the family's history and relationships. Lawrence's mom told me that she has a hard time with him at home, to put it mildly. Specifically, she said that he had "gone through" six television sets in his bedroom. This told me two things. First, he would get so upset at home, for whatever reason or motivation, that he would physically act out and break the television in his bedroom. Second, that his mother kept replacing the television, over and over and over again. Perhaps Lawrence did not have clear boundaries or consequences at home. I had also heard stories from other teachers about Lawrence's older sisters, who were about five years older. They told me that what I was seeing from Lawrence was much more severe with his older sisters and that he was likely not seeing positive behavioral role models at home. Maybe he did not feel a sense of belonging within the system of his family. Maybe his mistaken goal of misguided power actually worked well for him at home to feel a sense of connection with his family.

Whatever Lawrence went home to, I decided I could take concrete steps to make sure Lawrence felt secure boundaries and connected to the community at school. I reestablished my expectations for the whole class during school counselor lessons and encouraged Lawrence's classroom teacher to do the same, though I knew this would not be enough for him. I could see that Lawrence needed to feel power and attention by being singled out from the class while still needing to feel included among his peers. Lawrence's teacher and I started giving Lawrence jobs to do. Sometimes we would use iPads during school counselor lessons, so I asked Lawrence to help me wheel the iPad cart back to the classroom, just the two of us, after the lesson. He loved the personal attention, and I think pushing the heavy cart made him feel powerful (and expending some extra physical energy certainly did not hurt this energetic student, either).

Lawrence's teacher also gave me some great insight with the simplest of phrases: she told me, "He's a relationship kid." Suddenly, something else clicked for me. Lawrence didn't just need to feel powerful; he also needed to feel cared for. He was the baby of his family, and now in kindergarten, he was just one of a whole group of students and he did not feel the emotional connection he needed with the adults at school. In his classroom, he would go up to his teacher randomly throughout the day and lean into her for a hug. I spoke to him one day and let him know that if he ever felt like he needed a hug from me during a lesson, he could always ask for one, even during work time. I also started a new practice of asking Lawrence one get-to-know-you question every day. I think his favorite was, "What is your favorite superhero?" An enormous smile lit up his face when I asked, and he eagerly told me his favorite was Batman. Of course he loved superheroes, I thought to myself. They are powerful people who help their communities in meaningful ways.

I was making progress creating a relationship with Lawrence, but his behaviors during my school counselor lessons were not immediately improving. I worried that the whole class's social-emotional learning was suffering due to Lawrence's distracting behavior, so I decided to add a new strategy. I needed to find a way to proactively prevent him from becoming dysregulated; by the time he reached that level, he was virtually unreachable by any means I could ascertain. I mainly focused on his behavior on the carpet during the lesson introduction or read-aloud because that was when his behaviors were most interruptive to the class's learning. I pulled him out of class one day and explained to him my expectations and why I was asking him to sit crisscross and raise his hand to speak while on the carpet. Next, I said, "You know how superheroes sometimes have special, secret signals? Like, Batman has the bat signal that lights up the sky? I had an idea that you and I could make a special superhero signal for you. It would remind you to be your own kind of school superhero by following the rules in class. Does that sound like something you would like to do?" His smile split wide as he nodded emphatically. "So, we need to come up with something that I could do as a secret signal to you to remind you to sit quietly on the rug that no other kids would understand, just you. What do you think I could do?" This question seemed to stump him, though he still looked excited. I made a few suggestions of simple gestures. He picked tapping the side of my head with my pointer finger, the gesture that some people use generally to mean, "think."

During the next school counselor lesson, we tried our new system. I noticed the telltale signs that he was about to start misbehaving—looking around the room, fidgeting with his hands, rocking backward to lie on the ground. I made eye contact with him, gave him the tapping-head signal, and—to my amazement—he sat straight up, hands folded, eyes on me, smiling broadly. The secret superhero signal had worked! He and I were both very proud of our efforts.

Lawrence and I were making progress in our relationship, but I also felt it was important for him to feel a sense of belonging with his classmates. The greatest obstacle to his forming friendships was his unpredictable emotionality and physicality. Lawrence tended to deal with frustration or disappointment by throwing crayons or toys or sometimes by pushing or hitting classmates. This made his behavior unpredictable, and I noticed other students were starting to keep their distance from him during playtime. For Lawrence to feel a meaningful sense of belonging in his social world through positive actions rather than his misguided power-seeking goal, he needed to learn some essential emotional regulation skills. I taught him skills both through pull-out and push-in sessions. I taught him about belly breathing as a way to calm down, having him place a block on his belly while lying down so he could see it go up and down as his breath went in and out. Then I went to his classroom during playtime and coached him through the difficult moments. For example, once the "spaceship" he made from blocks broke while he was zooming it around the room. He immediately started crying and stomping his feet. I kneeled next to him and reminded him to take some deep breaths and to tell me how he was feeling. He told me he was sad because his spaceship broke. "Sometimes things break and it can make people feel sad. How do you think we could solve the problem?" I said. "Rebuild it?" he helpfully suggested, and I agreed this would be a great solution. We immediately got to work building a new spaceship.

Although Lawrence's emotional regulation skills were improving, he still seemed to be engaging in much more parallel play than cooperative play. Once again, I pushed into his room during work time and playtime to encourage his use of social skills to create positive interactions with peers. For example, during a coloring activity during which he tried to grab a crayon from his neighbor, I reminded him to ask nicely instead and encouraged the other student to share when asked. After a successful interaction, I asked him, "Doesn't it feel good to be kind?" He smiled and said "Yes." I hoped that he would feel powerful in his ability to affect the emotions of those around him—now by being kind instead of by being mean or disruptive. During playtime, when he was at his favorite station, the blocks, I suggested that he ask another student to play and wondered aloud if they could build something together and what they might like to build. I made sure to point out when Lawrence was sharing, using kind words, or keeping his body calm in an effort to build off of his strengths. Focusing on strengths is another aspect of Adlerian theory, and one that I thought particularly important for Lawrence, as it connected with his desire for power.

Over the next few months, the strategies designed to help Lawrence to feel cared for, to feel connected, and to feel an appropriate amount of power and leadership seemed to be helping some, although not completely, nor all the time. There were good days and tough days, and within a day there were good moments and tough moments. Considering what I knew of his family dynamics, I wanted to find more long-term support for Lawrence. I called his mom again and explained that we were fortunate enough to have a community therapist who worked with students during the school day. His mom was struggling with him at home. I sensed some hesitation from her, but after I explained the benefits Lawrence might receive from this type of support, she agreed that this was the right course of action. Lawrence began seeing the therapist for skills work around emotional regulation. When I checked in with the therapist, she told me that he loved the one-on-one time and that in her session plans she was focusing on emotional regulation skills using his favorite topic, superheroes. Things were still difficult sometimes with Lawrence, but I felt hopeful that maybe with the extra support, strategies, and adults in his corner, he could grow into the joyful, kind, brilliant student that I knew he could be.

At the end of the school year, I was faced with a new challenge with regard to Lawrence—termination. For a variety of reasons, I would no longer be working at Lawrence's school during the following school year. After all of my hard work building a relationship with Lawrence, I now contemplated how I would handle termination. Of all the kindergarten students, I was most worried about Lawrence's reaction because he and I had worked closely together and his emotional regulation skills still lagged behind his peers. I wanted to tell Lawrence before I told the rest of the kindergarteners to show respect for the relationship we had developed and because I thought he might react strongly if in a large group.

I knew that I needed to model a healthy way to address saying good-bye that would make sense to Lawrence at his developmental level. Once again, I turned to Lawrence's favorite topic, superheroes, to save the day. I decided to have a superhero-themed termination session inspired by Adlerian theory's emphasis on the child's strengths. I spoke to his teacher beforehand and pulled Lawrence out of class for a special one-on-one session in my room. Later that day, I would be telling all the kindergarteners that I would not be returning the following school year. I described to him how I had seen him grow this past year in superhero-type language—super listening skills, laser focus, emotional strength to calm down. I had made a paper with "Lawrence's Super Powers" at the top with pictures and words to echo what I was telling Lawrence verbally that I pointed to during our talk. When I was done sharing, I asked Lawrence if he had any superpowers he wanted to add to the list. "Super speed!" he enthusiastically suggested. Well, I thought, he definitely gets the superhero theme, though "super speed" was not one of the skills we focused on during the year. I rolled with his suggestion, though, and replied that recess was a great time for his super speed and that hallway and classroom times were for his "super calm body skills." I went on to explain that I had been like his sidekick this year, like Robin helping Batman, and now Batman was strong enough to practice his super skills himself. In more explicit language, I told him I would not be working at his school anymore, and that he would have a different school counselor the following year. I planned to tell the new school counselor that Lawrence might need more support, so I wanted to start building a bridge between him and the new school counselor even before he met her. I also explained that he would still be able to see the in-school therapist. I asked him a few questions to make sure he understood that I would not be his school counselor next year. He seemed to understand. He accepted all this information placidly enough and quickly moved on to talk about what was for snack that afternoon.

At that moment, I realized that although Lawrence did need a proper termination, I was feeling more emotional about it than he was. The loss of our relationship was not real to him in that moment. He could not developmentally conceptualize that abstract future, but I could. A red flag went off in my head; I needed a self-care boost. As a professional, I needed to take care of my own emotional needs so that my emotions did not interfere with my professional practice. Later that day, I called a school counselor friend of mine at another school to process with her the termination with Lawrence and my switching schools more generally.

Two years after my work with Lawrence ended, I received an update on Lawrence's progress. His behavior had shown considerable improvement between kindergarten and second grade. He had a few physical incidents in first grade but not nearly as many as in kindergarten and none at all in second grade. Though I did not receive any more details than that, in my mind I imagined him as his happy, bright, shining self, brimming with excitement at life's possibilities with his characteristic wide grin bubbling over into joyful laughter.

CASE DISCUSSION

Alfred Adler's four "mistaken goals" of misbehavior informed my understanding of Lawrence and his behavior. In particular, Adler discussed the four mistaken goals of attention seeking, power seeking, revenge seeking, and inadequacy as maladaptive efforts for children to attain belonging and contribution to their social world (Sweeney, 1989). Rudolf Dreikurs's (1964) *Children: The Challenge* translates Adler's theory into practical applications. Though this book is framed for parents, I found it useful as an adult working with children. Dreikurs (1964) emphasizes the importance of adults' consideration of children's goals, even if the goal or the child's efforts toward that goal may seem completely nonsensical. It is not helpful to simply dismiss a child's behavior as illogical or ridiculous. When adults take the child's perspective of the world, Dreikurs (1964) argues, they can more fully understand and help children. This framework reminded me to step out of my own shoes and into Lawrence's to consider his reality at school and at home, his role within the family and the class, and what he might ultimately want from his connections with others. I considered ways he could satisfy his desire for power while also satisfying what I suspected was an underlying need for meaningful social connection.

Adler also emphasized the importance of considering the whole family, including parents, in reflecting on a child's behavior (Dreikurs, 1964). Moreover, my conversations with Lawrence's mother were informed by my knowledge of the importance of parental involvement in children's education. Piko and Hamvai (2010) emphasized the connection between parent engagement and students' well-being. Another study found parent involvement to be most predictive of adolescent mental health of all the educational factors included in the study (Suldo, McMahan, Chappel, & Loker, 2012). I made sure to connect with Lawrence's mom early during my work with him. I believe these early contacts were instrumental in developing a trusting relationship between Lawrence's mom and me. This relationship made it possible for us to speak openly about what would be helpful for Lawrence, and I believe it was the reason she was open to the idea of Lawrence seeing the in-school therapist. In my experience, many parents are hesitant about therapy because of the stigma still associated with it, but her trust in my professional judgment and good intentions helped us overcome that barrier.

Much of my work with Lawrence was in an effort to improve his appropriate engagement with my school counselor lessons, both for his social-emotional learning and that of the rest of the class. This emphasis in my work with Lawrence exemplifies that my school counselor program prioritized classroom guidance lessons, which is in line with the American School Counselor Association's national model (American School Counselor Association [ASCA], 2012). The ASCA (2012) national model provides recommendations for the percentage of time that school counselors spend on each aspect of their program. ASCA's (2012) national model recommends school counselors spend 80 percent or more of their time on program delivery. In particular, it advises elementary school counselors to spend 35 to 40 percent of their "delivery" time on "guidance curriculum" (ASCA, 2012, p. 136), which is a higher percentage than that recommended for middle or high school levels. My extensive support of students through classroom lessons was in line with ASCA's recommended use-of-time percentages. Due to the higher percentage of time recommended for elementary-level school counselors to spend on classroom guidance lessons, I inferred this to be a particularly important part of a comprehensive elementary school counseling program according to the ASCA national model (2012). As such, I wanted my lessons to be as effective as possible for all students. When Lawrence's behavior began to improve (for example, through the use of our "secret signal"), there were fewer distractions for students, and I noticed all the students seemed more focused and engaged.

When I consider my work with Lawrence, I think about how Lawrence helped me become a better school counselor and highlighted ways I still desire to improve. An experienced teacher once told me that she was grateful to students like Lawrence for finding the flaws in the tier 1 systems, rituals, and routines and that wise educators take that opportunity to improve their systems class-wide so that all students' experiences are improved. Though I am not a classroom teacher, this case made me reflect on the way I conduct my classroom lessons. I continue to improve upon making my expectations clear; providing simple, concise, and thorough directions; and choosing engaging, fun lesson materials and activities.

My termination with Lawrence underscored to me the importance of school counselor self-care. Although I gave a great deal of thought to how I would provide Lawrence with appropriate closure and begin the groundwork for his relationship with the new school counselor, I did not give as much thought to my own reaction to the end of my time at that school. I realized after my conversation with Lawrence that perhaps my extensive concerns about how students would react to my decision to leave partially were born of my own sadness and anxiety about leaving the school. I found ways to process these emotions and support myself through this transition: I leaned on my school counselor colleagues across the school district, as well as my personal friends and family outside of my work world. I checked in on my self-care routines—maybe I could use a bit of extra sleep or some more time exercising outdoors. I remembered the expression, "You can pour only from a full cup" and made sure I was doing all I could to keep my cup full.

As I reflect on my experience with Lawrence, I come to one main conclusion: the power of relationships. The moments when Lawrence felt connected, seen, and valued, he thrived. I learned that sometimes little things, like asking a simple question every day, when thoughtfully done, made a difference. The hugs, secret signals, class jobs, and discussions about our favorite foods were verbal or physical manifestations of that invisible connection between human beings. Adlerian theory helped me make sense of Lawrence's behavior and create an organized plan to support him, but this would have been a hollow approach without our relationship at the core of all of our work together.

DISCUSSION QUESTIONS

1. In what other ways could the counselor have used Lawrence's love of superheroes to help him learn emotional regulation? Create a plan for a classroom, small-group, or individual activity related to the theme of superheroes.

2. How do you think the demographic context of Lawrence's school affected either his behavior or the counselor's response to his behavior?

3. Consider other aspects of Adlerian theory not discussed in this chapter (e.g., encouragement vs. discouragement, birth order, etc.) and apply it to this case study. How do these concepts impact your understanding of Lawrence or your opinion of the strategies used with him?

REFERENCES

American School Counselor Association (2012). The ASCA national model: A framework for school counselor programs (3rd ed.). Alexandria, VA: Author.

Dreikurs, R. (1964). *Children: The challenge.* New York, NY: Plume.

Piko, B. F., & Hamvai, C. (2010). Parent, school and peer-related correlates of adolescents' life satisfaction. *Children and Youth Services Review, 32,* 1479–82.

Positive Discipline (2018). *Mistaken goal chart.* Retrieved from www.positivediscipline.com/sites/default/files/mistakengoalchart.pdf.

Suldo, S. M., McMahan, M. M., Chappel, A. M., & Loker, T. (2012). Relationships between perceived school climate and adolescent mental health across genders. *School Mental Health, 4*(2), 69–80.

Sweeney, T. J. (1989). *Adlerian counseling: A practical approach to a new decade* (3rd ed.). Muncie, IN: Accelerated Development.

Chapter Five

Dara

This case study is inspired from early in my counseling career when I served middle school students in a well-off suburb of a major metropolitan area. The school district served mostly white, Christian middle- and upper-class families. The school is a junior high school containing eighth and ninth grades. Although the school district has a comfortable amount of financial resources, the student–to–school counselor ratio is 650:1. The school has only one school counselor who is in the building full-time and another who splits work among the district's multiple elementary schools and junior high.

As you read this case study, look for the following:

- Relational-cultural approach (Jordan, 2010) that informs the Aderlian theoretical orientation when working with students and their families
- Strategies for building the working alliance
- Ways that the counselor provides care for the entire system of people that surrounds the student

CASE STUDY INTRODUCTION

This case study reflects on work I did with Dara to support her to feel connected both at school and in her adoptive home. Dara was a fourteen-year-old eighth grade student who was adopted at age twelve along with her younger biological sister. They were abandoned by their mother, who dropped them off at an orphanage and never returned. Dara experienced challenging treatment in the orphanage center, often being neglected by the overtaxed care workers. Most of the other children at the center were babies and toddlers who were there because their parents died, but Dara was older, abandoned at age eight. I learned about Dara prior to the beginning of the school year. Her mother had called because she wanted to get to know the counselors and make sure we would have time for her daughter.

INCIDENT

"Hello, this is Sarah, Brookridge Park School counselor."

"Yes, hi. My name is Cynthia Jones. I am calling about my daughter who is an incoming student at your school. Her name is Dara. I know you counselors have too many students to attend to. I want to make sure you know about my daughter because she will likely end up in your office for disciplinary reasons. I adopted her two years ago with her sister. Her sister is fine, but Dara has me at the end of my rope. I want to make sure she doesn't do that to you, too. It's exhausting."

I first made mental note of Dara's older age of adoption, as well as the fact that she was adopted along with a biological sibling. Those were helpful details for me as I conceptualized what life might be like for Dara. I then informed her mother about my role as a school counselor. It's a value of our profession to not be the disciplinarians; rather, we support the students' well-being. Yes, we have large caseloads, which is an unfortunate truth of the state we live in, as helping professions in the schools are underfunded. I told her the good news is that I always have had large caseloads, so I've gotten pretty good at learning how to create some type of relationship with my students even if I don't know most of them well. I briefly stated that we have a comprehensive school counseling program, which means that 80 percent of my work is devoted to direct work with students—most of which involves working one-on-one with students.

"Great, well my Dara is a handful and is not very kind. Don't take it personally. We adopted children thinking we could make a difference, but frankly, this has been far more difficult than I ever imagined."

Even though Dara would be a student on my caseload, I recognized that her mother was the one to whom I was speaking. My priority is service to my students. One of the ways I provide care for my students is also by creating open, caring relationships with their caregivers. By supporting the environment my students exist in at home, I indirectly also support the student. I turned the focus of the phone call to the mother's distress.

"I hear that parenting Dara has felt overwhelming. I'm glad you called so we could connect. Communication between the two of us will be important as we support Dara's success and well-being. Is there anything specific I can do for you now?"

"No, no. I just wanted to make personal contact. Thank you for your time."

After the phone call I walked to my colleague's office; he split his time at the elementary school and likely knew of Dara and her family. I learned that Dara and her sister spent four years in a Catholic orphanage in Southeast Asia. It sounded like Dara's sister was truly thriving both academically and socially, but Dara was quick to become irritable toward teachers and peers.

My colleague sighed as he used his hands to make air quotes as he described Dara as a "problem student." Apparently, there were multiple meetings in the past among administrators, teachers, and her parents to help her treat her peers with respect. She would be overcome with anger and have outbursts. I empathized with him, noting that it sounded like he took a lot of time to help support Dara and her family.

Once the school year began, it wasn't long before I met Dara. It was just the second day of school and I was on morning duty, walking through the cafeteria as students arrived at school before the first class began. Although the room echoed with the loud chatter of the adolescents and has uncomfortable florescent lighting, I enjoyed days on morning duty. I sipped my coffee and got a good pulse on how most students were doing. I would try to tell who was feeling socially well-adjusted and who could use a smiling face. I always took the time to smile or say hi to the students who seemed to be having it rough that day.

I ran into Dara in the corner of the cafeteria. Her long dark hair was slightly unkempt in a low ponytail. She was raising her voice at some peers and lifted her hand as if she was going to strike them. Quickly intervening, I positioned my body between Dara and her peers.

"Good morning!" I said, both half-smiling to appear friendly but also furrowing my brow to match Dara's concerned expression. "It looks like you're feeling upset."

"They asked me to slide down to make room for more people!" Dara exclaimed.

I looked over at the other students to understand the context of the situation. They sat, wide-eyed, appearing surprised that a simple request escalated so quickly. I looked back at Dara, who was red in the face. It appeared her anger was expanding. The bell rang, prompting students to go to their first period. Dara quickly jolted her body toward the students as they got up, as if she were about to pounce on them at any moment.

"Come with me to my office," I stated in an inviting tone. Dara was clearly agitated. Telling her to "brush it off" and send her to class likely would not have been helpful. It was obvious that—to her—somebody did something that was disrespectful toward her.

As we arrived at my office, she looked around, seeing the board games I had on my shelf, the art supplies I set out on my table, and the various fidgets and knickknacks I had in a bowl.

"Hi, I'm Sarah. Welcome. When we're in here, you can play with whatever you'd like. I'll let you know if there is anything you cannot do. What's your name?"

"Dara," she said gruffly.

I was unclear at that point if she still was worked up from the cafeteria incident or if she was irritated with me for inviting her to my office. Since my caseload was so large and I had limited time with students, I practiced a condensed form of Adlerian counseling, moving on to each phase rather quickly. It wasn't always ideal but it was the best I could do.

Working from an Adlerian perspective, the first priority or phase of counseling is establishing a relationship. Before asking Dara more about her anger in the cafeteria or about ways I could be helpful, I wanted to use attending skills and empathetic listening to show Dara I desired to meet her where she was at.

Dara sat at my small table with the art supplies. She picked up a black marker and started to draw.

"You've decided to draw," I stated, tracking her behavior so she knew I was paying attention.

There was some silence. The silence helped Dara calm down, and I didn't want to fill up the space too quickly. I wanted to see what was on her mind first.

After what felt like ten minutes to me but was probably only ten seconds, she stated, "They don't understand."

"They?" I encouraged her to elaborate on whom she was talking about with this one word paired with my curious facial expression.

"Everybody. I cannot wait until I can go back home." She was looking at her paper as she drew lines. It appeared to me she was drawing a stick figure. I noticed the figure she was drawing was rudimentary for her age.

"Where is home for you?"

"Micronesia. My grandparents are waiting for me there." She set the marker down and picked up some of the fidgets. Instead of playing with their mechanics and moving parts, she started to line them up on the table in a straight line. I noted that like her drawing, lining up toys was something I expected from a young child instead of a middle schooler.

I realized Dara was already trusting me and opening up. I switched my mind-set to the second phase of Adlerian counseling: understanding Dara's psychological dynamics, investigating what was meaningful to her, and conceptualizing who she was as a holistic person.

I asked her the question that would help me get to know Dara's goals, "Suppose you woke up tomorrow and something magic happened: every problem in your life was solved. When waking up, what would be different in your life?"

She kept lining up the toys without looking up. "I would be back in Micronesia, living with my grandparents. My mother would be there, too. My sister and I would be happy. We would have food to eat, and my mother would have a job, so she wouldn't have to bring us to the orphanage again."

Although from my personal perspective, Dara's answer was quite unrealistic, from my theoretical understanding, it is not my purpose to tell her how unlikely her answer was. Instead, I used her answer to inform my understanding of her. It was clear that her goals were (1) to be united with biological family and (2) to feel a sense of security for her basic needs. My role was to help her clarify these values and identify actions she could take to move toward them.

"It sounds like family is important to you."

Dara nodded.

"Tell me about your earliest memories of family."

Dara recalled memories of her and her mother together asking for money on the streets while her grandparents took care of her younger sister. She recalled these memories with fondness, smiling and lighting up as she spoke about adventures with her mother. It was evident that Dara felt happy as a child, which was markedly different from the angry girl in front of me now. No wonder: from her perspective, she was separated from her family and forced to move to the other side of the world. She did not seem to have a narrative that she was abandoned by her mother; instead she seemed to have a story of forced separation due to economic hardship and of hope of one day being united again.

I noted Dara's hope of reunification with her family. Over time, I wanted to use Dara's optimism for unity to help her develop strong relationships.

"How do you cope not being with family now?"

"I tell everyone how mad I am. Everyone acts all happy all the time. If I can make them mad, too, then maybe they'll understand I need to go home."

My heart ached with her. I felt the significant loss and separation. Dara was not a "problem student." She was lonely and mad about circumstances that forever changed her life.

"Everyone acts happy," I reflected.

"Yeah. They tell me how I should act and think I should be happy all the time. But I'm not."

"I heard you say they 'think you should be happy all the time.' What are some alternative explanations?" I was attempting to help Dara develop some perceptual alternatives—that is, other ideas about what might be happening around her.

"What?" Dara asked.

I remembered Dara's immature drawing and lining up of toys. Concrete wording would probably be most effective with Dara. "When people want you to be happy, they might be thinking, 'you should be happy all the time.'

They might also be thinking other things. What are other thoughts they could be thinking?"

Dara sat in silence, appearing deep in thought. She did not break the silence.

"What are you thinking about as we sit here together?"

"Cynthia."

"Cynthia often tries to make you happy?"

"She tries to do everything for me and tells me I should be happy. But she doesn't understand. She is a bad woman."

Before asking more questions, I make sure to empathize with Dara first. "Cynthia does a lot for you, but you don't like her."

"Yeah!"

Moving to the third phase of Adlerian counseling, using psychological interpretation of what's going on around her, I decided to help Dara come up with a perceptual alternative to test a hypothesis I had.

"Dara, earlier today you mentioned that family is very important to you. It seems to me that for you, Cynthia is not part of your family. However, could it be that Cynthia also values family and that for her, you are part of her family?"

"She will never be my family."

It seemed that Dara wasn't ready for alternative perspectives. I respected that and learned from my hypothesis testing that Dara truly feels out of place here. "Here" being with her adoptive family but also likely in this school and community. Although it would be unrealistic to get to it today, I was gaining an understanding of where the counseling work would be for Dara, which was the fourth phase of Adlerian theory: reorientation and reeducation.

I arranged to meet with Dara ongoing as her academic schedule allowed. Over time, my goals were to help Dara gain awareness and insight into the kind of life she wanted and to use that awareness as motivation to find functional behaviors to reach her goals. Her goals were to feel a sense of belonging. Once she had an understanding that she felt she belonged with her biological family but not with anyone here in the United States, we worked to gain motivation to create healthy relationships. She developed the belief that practicing positive relationships at school would help her develop skills to have positive relationships with her grandparents when she moved back to Micronesia as an adult. In the little time we had together, we worked to identify skills that help create relationships and foster a sense of belonging.

I did not hear about Dara after she moved to the high school and I moved on to other professional positions away from that district. I still think about her now that she is older than eighteen. I wonder what life has brought her and if she's been in touch with her grandparents or returned to Micronesia. I have the utmost hope for her to develop relationships where she feels she belongs.

CASE DISCUSSION

I conceptualize the nature of my counseling work from both Adlerian and ecological systems theories (Adler, 1930; Bronfenbrenner, 1977, 1994). Clinically speaking, Adlerian principles emphasize individual social context and external dynamics (Adler, 1930), which inform me to pay attention to the contextual variables of the students with whom I work. I pay attention to each student's norms, values, family structure, and culture, as well as their unique individual and personality characteristics. After all, being a new student at a school can look incredibly different if a student is energetic, talkative, and coming from a supportive household versus introspective, slow to open up, or coming from a household with parents who are anxious or depressed.

I also understand my work through ecological systems theory (Bronfenbrenner, 1994). School counselors exist within systems of schools, districts, and communities. I function in these complex systems to benefit student development. School counselors can exist in a student's microsystem, having direct contact with students, yet they also function in the mesosystem when interacting with parents and guardians, which can have positive, yet indirect benefits for the student (Bronfenbrenner, 1994; Warren & Baker, 2013). When considering school counseling policy, school counseling also exists in the student's exosystem. In this case example, the district's policy that set the student–to–school counselor ratio had an impact on the direct services Dara received.

Using Adlerian theory provides me foundational principles that inform my work. A central value of this approach is holding a positive view of human nature. I conceptualize clients optimistically, focusing on their capability for resilience, growth, and resourcefulness (Corey, 2009). Because of her challenging behaviors, it was easy to view Dara as a "problem" who couldn't follow the norms of the school system or respect her adoptive parents. I'll admit that if I were her teacher or adoptive guardian, I probably would have an extremely difficult time, too. As her counselor, I was afforded the gift of viewing her outside of those everyday environments.

Furthermore, I span my positive view of human nature to the other people in the system. Instead of becoming irritated with my colleague and the teachers who described Dara as a "problem student," I chose empathy with him that acknowledged how difficult his job was and how supporting Dara made his job more difficult. There are no "good" or "bad" reactions, just human reactions that help us understand what is happening. The reactions of everyone around helped me understand how significant Dara's anger and loneliness was. If her emotion was so significant that she was being disruptive everywhere she went, I can only imagine how big it felt inside of her.

The positive view of human nature informs every phase of support I provide. The four phases of Adlerian work are: (1) establishing a relationship, (2) understanding the client's psychological dynamics, (3) psychological interpretation, and (4) reorientation and reeducation (Corey, 2009). Although typically these phases span multiple sessions in a traditional counseling setting, in a school setting where the school counselor balances multiple demands and responsibilities, these phases can be condensed, even into one or two short meetings. In the incident dialogue, you can see where I cognitively switched from working in one phase to the next. It can appear different for each student. In this case, Dara was quick to connect with me and open up, which helped me advance to the later phases rather quickly.

Another key component of Adlerian theory is its emphasis on a person's ability to adapt to feeling inferior (Adler, 1924). For Dara, it seemed that she felt she could contribute to her biological family's well-being and way of life. In other words, she felt adequate in her childhood. Yet as she was separated from her biological family, she felt inadequate—or inferior— trapped in a life she didn't choose for herself. Her persistent feelings of inferiority from the moment her mother left her surmounted to anger and frustration. She moved to a new country and became part of an adoptive family in which her livelihood and expectations greatly changed. She had no outlet for empowered action to pour her inferior feelings into. It seemed that Dara used aggression to try to socially dominate those around her. Doing so gave her a feeling of power and control amid circumstances that were out of her control. My goal for Dara was to find sense of empowerment by helping her clarify her values and goals. Upon gaining a clearer idea of what was important to her, she would have direction to channel her actions, helping her feel more adequate as a person.

One of the most important takeaways for me as Dara's counselor was a greater understanding of my role compared to the power of a person's context. I was a shiny new counselor who had the energy and ideals to make an impact on all of my students that would transform their lives. Dara's social context contained multiple significant stressors, and I quickly learned that my role was simply to be a trusted adult who did not add more stress to her life. I had to "set down" my ideals that the work I did with Dara would "fix" her difficulties fitting in socially and connecting with her adoptive mother. As soon as I took away the big responsibility of becoming Dara's savior, I was able to meet her where she was and accept her for who she was.

I also learned when to check my assumptions and narrow Euro-American lens. Frankly, who was I to tell her that she couldn't move back to Micronesia as an adult? Sure, assumptions and biases came to mind such as, "Do her grandparents want her to move back as she claims?" and "She has such an opportunity here in the United States to get education and create a life for herself." These thoughts perpetuate stereotypes and assumptions that inhibit my ability to effectively work with Dara. I had to learn to join her where she was at and help her to craft her own goals and motivations. Her motivations were family and economic stability. Helping her clarify those goals and decide on actions that help her move toward them will allow her to continually evaluate her life.

DISCUSSION QUESTIONS

1. What internal reactions do you have toward the people in this case?
2. How would these internal reactions help or hurt the way you view Dara?
3. Is the counseling work worth it, even though no measurable improvement was observed by the counselor in this case?
4. Considering what you know about Adlerian theory, is there anything that you would have done differently than the counselor?

REFERENCES

Adler, A. (1924). *The practice and theory of individual psychology* (P. Radin, Trans.). London: Routledge, Trench, Trubner & Co.
Adler, A. (1930). *The education of children.* (E. Jensen & F. Jensen, Trans.). South Bend, IN: Gateway Editions.
Bronfenbrenner, U. (1977). Toward an experimental ecology of human development. *American Psychologist, 32*, 513–31.
Bronfenbrenner, U. (1994). Ecological models of human development. In *International Encyclopedia of Education*, Vol. 3, 2nd ed. Oxford: Elsevier. Reprinted in Guavain, M. & Cole, M. (Eds.), Readings on the development of children, 2nd ed. (1993, pp. 37–43). New York, NY: Freeman.
Corey, G. (2009). *Theory and practice of counseling and psychotherapy.* Belmont, CA: Brooks/Cole.
Jordan, J. V. (2010). *Relational-cultural therapy.* Washington, DC: American Psychological Association
Warren, J. M., & Baker, S. B. (2013). School counselor consultation: Enhancing teacher performance through rational emotive-social behavioral consultation. *Vistas, 69*, 1–15.

Chapter Six

Damaris

The school counselor in this case study is in her third year of practice in a high school setting, with two additional years of experience at the middle school level. The counselor primarily uses brief counseling approaches (e.g., solution-focused brief therapy). However, when necessary, she utilizes counseling approaches that are a better fit for the student's needs and cultural background, such as the Adlerian approach. The setting is a Title I school in Florida with approximately 80 percent of the population qualifying for free or reduced lunch. The ethnicities in the school include 55 percent Latino, 30 percent black, 10 percent white, and 5 percent other.

As you read this case study, look for the following:

- Cues as to why Adlerian theory was chosen as the theoretical foundation
- How a multicultural counseling approach was used in addition to Adlerian tenets
- The stages of Adlerian therapy and how they can be applied in a school setting
- Specific Adlerian techniques that can be used with adolescents

CASE STUDY INTRODUCTION

Damaris is a fourteen-year-old ninth grader who identifies as female and uses the pronouns she/her/hers. Damaris's grandparents came to the United States from South America when her mother was a teenager. She was born in the United States and has lived in Florida her whole life. Damaris has never known her father; she lives with her mother and grandparents and has no siblings. According to Damaris her family is "middle class" and "very religious." She shares that they closely adhere to Catholicism. She speaks Spanish fluently and enjoys holidays in which her family celebrates her South American heritage. Damaris is a bright and engaged student, especially in classes that are related to the arts, music, and history. Damaris sings in the school choir and has many friends, many whom are also Latino.

INCIDENT

The choir director, Mr. Winston (Mr. W.), referred Damaris to me because he noticed a significant change in her demeanor. Mr. W. shared that Damaris used to be more upbeat and enthusiastic in choir, but for the past few weeks he noticed a decline in her energy level. The day prior, Mr. W. saw Damaris crying with a friend after choir practice and said that she seemed distraught. Mr. W. inquired what was wrong, and because they had a good relationship, Damaris disclosed that she has a close friend whom her family does not approve of, and it was causing her distress. Mr. W. asked Damaris if she would be willing to talk with the school counselor and she agreed. Mr. W. believes the main concern is a conflict between family expectations and her social life. He said that Damaris's family was supportive and loving, but, in his opinion, the family required her to follow strict rules compared with most students her age. For example, Mr. W. shared that Damaris has had to opt out of several choir performances that required an overnight stay because her family could not travel with her.

Because of the background information Mr. W. shared, I decided to conduct the counseling sessions through an Adlerian lens. This approach is culturally sensitive, focuses on encouragement, and involves discussion of family themes and the social environment (Aslinia, Rasheed, & Simpson, 2011).

In the first session with Damaris, I focused on the first two stages of Adlerian counseling, establishing rapport and understanding the client (Caterino & Sullivan, 2009; Sommers-Flanagan & Sommers-Flanagan, 2015). My initial aim was to create a warm and nonjudgmental environment. I learned that Damaris never worked with a counselor in the past. Her only interaction with the school counseling program was listening to the counselors' presentations during classes and having them help her decide on her coursework each year. Due to her limited counseling experiences, I made sure to discuss her expectations of our meetings and we carefully reviewed confidentiality. We went over a brief informed consent form that she would take home to have signed by her parent. This led to a discussion about concerns regarding what I would disclose to her mom.

Once confidentiality and the counseling process was clarified, I focused on learning about Damaris's culture, family, upbringing, friends, and what she enjoys in life. I asked general open-ended questions about what she would like me to know about her, as opposed to approaching the first session from a more directive approach (Sommers-Flanagan & Sommers-Flanagan, 2015). I did this with the intent of encouraging Damaris to lead the conversation and to take an active role in the counseling session. I intentionally focused on reflecting her strengths during this process. Some strengths I noticed included her close relationship with her family, a solid academic standing, strong work ethic, and loyalty to friends. This aligns with Adlerian tenets that clients are more resilient and empowered if counselors focus on their skills and strengths as opposed to their deficits (Hamm, Carlson, & Erguner-Tekinalp, 2016).

During the initial phase of counseling, I noticed some strong cultural themes emerging. Damaris shared a strong connection with her family and deep appreciation for their sacrifices and hard work. Her grandparents gave up everything in their native country to create a new life that would provide many more opportunities for her mother, and therefore for Damaris, as well. She expressed her family's strong belief in their religion, Catholicism. Although she enjoyed going to church with her family, Damaris shared that she did not truly believe in some of her family's religious beliefs. Damaris shared some challenges of going to school with peers whose families had lived in the United States much longer than her own. Damaris's friends typically came from families that encouraged independence and dream seeking. However, Damaris shared that her own family encouraged her to revolve her choices around the family and expected her to stay home as much as possible.

From Damaris's initial sharing, I heard some Adlerian themes including social interest and striving for superiority. Of importance to note is that the term of *superiority* in Adler's approach is often misinterpreted. Superiority does not refer to the pursuit of one's self-interest but rather one's pursuit of completeness (Aslinia, Rasheed, & Simpson, 2011; Sommers-Flanagan & Sommers-Flanagan, 2015). Damaris demonstrated that she held values and connection to her family, but she was also trying to find a way to feel complete through a connection with her social group. This all linked to Damaris's "style of life," the schema she held from her childhood experiences that helps her navigate life experiences, including her friendships (Sommers-Flanagan & Sommers-Flanagan, 2015).

After spending about thirty minutes learning about Damaris's background during this first session, it was important also to begin the process of clarifying her goals for future sessions. Below is a summary of the remainder of the first session:

Me: Thank you so much for sharing about yourself and your life. Before sending you back to class, I want to make sure we talk a bit about your goals for working with me. I'm hearing that overall you like being at school, but you have some struggles between what your family expects, what your friends expect, and what you want in life. Would you agree with that?

Damaris: Yeah . . . I feel like no matter what I decide, I can't make everyone happy. Especially myself, I guess [looking down]. I just don't know what to do.

Me: It sounds like you have something specific that you're struggling with.

Damaris: Yes . . . [fidgeting with her bracelets].

Me: I know it can be difficult to talk about things that are bothering us. But remember what I shared about confidentiality earlier. I only share what you tell me if I have reason to believe you might be in danger to yourself or others.

Damaris: Yeah, I don't want anyone to know what I'm going through. Except maybe one of my friends who knows.

Me: Tell me about this friend.

Damaris: We are really close and have been friends for about a year. She's in choir with me and we have so much fun together. I like her a lot.

Me: It sounds like she makes you happy.

Damaris: She does and that's part of the problem.

Me: How's that?

Damaris: [long pause] My family wouldn't like it. I think I like her a little too much.

Me: Like more than a friend?

Damaris: Yeah, I think so.

Damaris continued to share that she has had deeper feelings for her friend ever since they met. Damaris was at the point at which she could no longer ignore these feelings, and her friend has admitted to having deeper feelings for Damaris, as well. Her friend, Camila, identifies as lesbian and has had girlfriends in the past. Camila and Damaris have kissed on a few occasions and talked about their feelings for each other. Damaris shared that she felt guilty about her connection with Camila. She knew her family would deeply disapprove, as they have taught her that homosexuality is wrong. At this point, I wanted to better understand Damaris's goals to help provide some direction to the future counseling sessions.

Me: It sounds like you are struggling with the conflict between what you would like your relationship to look like with this friend and what your family expects of you.

Damaris: I think about it all the time and it makes me feel like crap. I get happy thinking about her, and then I think about my family, it immediately makes feel awful and my stomach hurts.

Me: That must be really tough to have that on your mind all the time. Have you ever experienced this in the past?

Damaris: No, not really. I mean, I don't always agree with my family because they're so strict, but usually I can deal with it. But this is different.

Me: I'm wondering if you have a goal you'd like to work on during our meetings together?

Damaris: I guess I just want to figure out what to do. Like should I be with this friend and just hide it from my family? Or should I just end it with her? Telling my family isn't an option since I know what they will say.

Me: And what is that?

Damaris: They will make me stop spending time with her. They may even make me drop out of choir since we have it together. They won't understand. There's no way I can tell them and be honest.

Me: It sounds like you are looking for a way to feel complete and happy while navigating your family expectations and your relationships.

Damaris: You could say that. It's probably impossible but I do want to talk more about it.

Me: Let's make that the focus of our work together then. We can focus on exploring what you want in life and in your relationships and also how you can do this in light of your family's expectations. From what I know about you so far, it sounds like you have a lot of strengths that will help you do this. You are connected to both your family and friends, and although you may not agree with everything they believe, you value, love, and respect them all.

Damaris: I definitely do.

At this point, we wrapped up the first session and planned for the second session. One important point to note is that at this point in the counseling process, it was my impression that the client came from a collectivist culture and family, yet she felt inclined to do some self-exploration, which could potentially lead to feelings of guilt. I also recognized the importance of paying attention to her acculturation strategy. It was my impression that the client wanted to pursue biculturalism, the integration of her family's culture with the culture of her friends (Nguyen & Benet-Martínez, 2013). I made an intentional effort to create a nonjudgmental environment in which the client could explore her style of life through her own lifestyle lens, whether it be collective, individual, or a combination of both (Aslinia, Rasheed, & Simpson, 2011).

After this first session I connected Damaris's presenting concerns to Adlerian tasks. According to Adler, individuals work toward mastering the three tasks of love, work, and community (Caterino & Sullivan, 2009). In Damaris's case, her current concerns focus on love and community. However, without attention to these two tasks, her work task could become problematic as well. Mr. W. noted that Damaris was participating less in choir and although her grades remained stable, if her love and community tasks were not attended to, it was likely her schoolwork would eventually suffer. Although our future sessions primarily focused on her personal and family relationship concerns, one overarching aim of our counseling sessions was to prevent academic issues from arising.

During the second phase of counseling with Damaris, I continued to try to understand her style of life and how she views the world. Damaris is an only child, and according to Adlerian theory, children with no siblings tend to be able to communicate effectively with adults (Caterino & Sullivan, 2009). This was apparent in the counseling sessions, as Damaris was extremely verbal and did not have difficulties explaining her thoughts or feelings. It was my impression that Damaris's pressure to live up to family expectations may be stronger since she is an only child. Another important element in Damaris's style of life was that she seemed to come from a home with healthy parent-child communication. Although her family could be perceived as being rule-focused, Damaris expressed that they always communicated reasons behind the rules, which typically centered around concerns for her safety. However, occasionally authoritative practices were mentioned in which the family laid down rules, such as an early curfew or no choir trips, without a clear explanation or opportunity to negotiate. This may have been difficult for Damaris to navigate, because according to Adlerian parent education tenets, it is important to modify parenting techniques with teenagers as they are attempting to gain more freedom and responsibility (Croake, 1983). This style-of-life concept impacted her work with Damarius as it also relates to the beliefs she has been taught about homosexuality and religion. According to Damaris, these views were taught without clear explanations or reasons behind the beliefs.

During this phase, we also discussed the Adlerian therapy technique called "the question" (Sommers-Flanagan & Sommers-Flanagan, 2015). I asked Damaris, "How would your life look different if your social life and family's expectations were not in conflict with each other?" This question was difficult for Damaris to answer at first, but she began picturing what being more open with her family would look like. She explained how she would be able to have more conversations with her family about things that are important to her. This helped me understand that Damaris avoided voicing her thoughts and ideas to her family, possibly because she felt pressured to achieve and meet their expectations.

In the next phase of counseling, I worked with Damaris on developing some insight about her situation. Insight and interpretation is the third phase of Adlerian therapy; during this phase, the counselor focuses on helping students better understand their thoughts and behaviors (Caterino & Sullivan, 2009). To help spark this conversation, we talked about a few beliefs that Damaris holds that differ from her family's beliefs. The first belief that we discussed was her family's guidelines and rules that they require Damaris to follow. Damaris believed these rules were too rigid and need updating. She would say things like, "This isn't 1950! Fourteen-year-olds don't have to be home by dinnertime anymore!" These rigid guidelines caused Damaris a lot of stress and although she followed her family's rules the majority of the time, she internalized feelings of anger about being held to stricter rules than those of her friends. Damaris would make statements such as, "My family doesn't care about me; they just want to control me." During the insight phase, it is important to collaboratively explore these beliefs and I asked questions like, "Is that true? Your family doesn't care about you?" Damaris recognized during this phase that her family does care about her, but due to their own cultural background, as well as their fears, their guidelines were strict. She also discussed that her family was afraid of what might happen to Damaris and regularly reminded her that "she is their only child and grandchild." Damaris gained some insight and understanding as to the reasons behind her family's strict rules, and I believe this helped her to be more accepting of these rules. We also discussed how some of these rules are only temporary as she is approaching early adulthood, and Damaris expressed some relief in talking about this as well.

The discussion about rules and guidelines was less complicated than the one about her family's religious beliefs regarding homosexuality. Damaris made it clear that she strongly disagreed with her family's views on homosexuality, which was especially distressing as she was considering exploring a same-sex romantic relationship. Damaris expressed concerns that if her family found out, they would probably make their rules even more rigid and possibly would disown her. She was worried she would have to suppress these feelings forever and could not be her true self with her family. Damaris expressed feelings of hopelessness, especially because she did not think her family would ever change their views.

To help Damaris process this, I asked her to write her "future autobiography" (Sommers-Flanagan & Sommers-Flanagan, 2015). In this narrative, Damaris wrote about what her life could look like. She was directed to write the story as if neither she nor her family was perfect. However, the story should be grounded in a world in which Damaris felt loved and felt a sense of belonging. Damaris's story helped her gain insight into a future world where she could find a place where she felt loved and accepted even though some of her beliefs conflicted with her family's beliefs. This story was not simple for Damaris to write as there were many unknowns. However, she processed what her life would look like if she were able to explore this relationship with her friend, most likely hiding this side of herself from her family. Damaris shared that this would feel unnatural because she had been open with her family in the past. However, she said that was a sacrifice she was willing to make so that she could figure out how she truly felt about her friend. In sharing her future story, Damaris talked about how she does not think she is a "true lesbian," because she tends to love people for whom they are, regardless of their gender. She said there was no way her family could understand that and does not think they ever will. However, Damaris recognized that there were ways that she could have romantic and sexual feelings about another person without her family knowing the depths of her feelings for this person. Ultimately, one insight I think that emerged from her autobiography was that Damaris acknowledged that her family would love her no matter what, even though they might disagree about whom she chose to love.

Reorientation and application is the final phase of Adlerian counseling. During this phase, the counselor helps the student identify alternative ways of thinking and behaving so a healthier lifestyle can be developed (Caterino & Sullivan, 2009). Damaris and I discussed how she typically viewed the world through an either/or perspective through her family's belief system or her friend's belief system (Nguyen & Benet-Martínez, 2007). We processed how it could help her to instead view the world through a both/and perspective in which she could accept and appreciate both her friends' cultural beliefs as well as her family's beliefs. Research demonstrates that a bicultural, both/and model may be helpful for individuals struggling with adjustment (Nguyen & Benet-Martínez, 2013).

Keeping the concept of biculturalism in mind, one technique I used during this phase was to encourage Damaris to act "as if" she could live in a world where these two cultures could exist in harmony with each other (Sommers-Flanagan & Sommers-Flanagan, 2015). We reflected on how that would look differently for her. Damaris talked about how she would not get upset so often. To help her act "as if," we processed what happened when Damaris got upset. She shared that in these moments, usually she thought about how her family would reject her if they found out she's interested in having a girlfriend. Damaris was able to come up with a different way of thinking about this, which was, "I don't even know if I will be in a same-sex relationship long term, and now I'm just exploring. Worrying about my family's reaction is premature right now. I have time to sort this out." We talked about how it would take more time and processing of her feelings to figure out what Damaris wanted her relationships to look like in the future.

Damaris and I met three times during which we had longer sessions of individual counseling (approximately fifty minutes each). After that, we decided to check in once a week for about twenty minutes. During those check-ins I wanted to determine whether to refer Damaris to long-term counseling. Damaris's demeanor significantly improved over the course of three to four weeks, and Mr. W. reported that her energy returned in choir. During our check-ins, Damaris shared that although she felt better overall, she still struggled internally because she felt her family could never understand her. She was still exploring her relationship with her friend, and though it had not developed into a serious relationship, Damaris was still deciding on her sexual orientation. She asked me about sexual identity terminology, so we spent time discussing and researching the difference between bisexuality and pansexuality. Damaris seemed energized when talking about these terms and wanted to explore more, but her main concern was still her family's reaction.

Because of this continued concern about her family, I asked Damaris for permission to talk to her mom and refer them to family therapy. We discussed what I would share with her mom so that Damaris would feel comfortable. Unfortunately, her mom worked during school hours, so we set up a phone call rather than an in-person meeting. Damaris was present for the call and we put her mom on speakerphone. Her mom was receptive to the family referral and agreed to pursue it. In future check-ins with Damaris, I learned that they went to several family sessions and that it seemed to help. Damaris was able to talk to her mom about feeling split between her friends' world and her world with her family. Damaris did not bring up any issues related to her sexuality during family counseling, but she said the sessions helped her feel more comfortable talking with her mom overall.

I continued to check in with Damaris throughout the remaining five or six months of school. Her demeanor seemed more upbeat, her academics remained stable, and our individual check-ins focused primarily on her thoughts related to her exploration of her sexual identity. At one point, I referred Damaris to a support group in the community for questioning youth but she declined due to concerns that her family would find out. Damaris shared that family counseling helped, and she went with her mom about once every two weeks.

CASE DISCUSSION

I was grateful that Mr. W. brought Damaris's situation to my attention because it is challenging for a school counselor to identify students who are academically stable yet in need of proactive counseling supports to prevent academic problems from arising. Without counseling supports, Damaris would have few resources to help her navigate her challenges and therefore could become more emotionally unstable, which could eventually impact her academic standing as well. Once I learned the root of Damaris's concerns, I recognized the strong need to provide her with supports since LGBTQ (lesbian, gay, bisexual, transgender, queer, and questioning) adolescents are at risk for depression and suicidal ideation (Baams, Grossman, & Russell, 2015). This need is even more significant for minority youths. I decided on using an Adlerian approach with this student as it is preventative, focuses on encouraging the client, and addresses maladaptive thoughts and behaviors while also bringing in systemic elements related to the family, society, and culture. Additionally, the Adlerian approach has been found to be applicable to collectivist cultures and enabled me to incorporate multicultural concepts such as biculturalism. (Aslinia, Rasheed, & Simpson, 2011; Nguyen & Benet-Martínez, 2007).

Although providing long-term therapy to a student would be inappropriate, this short-term therapy helped me to work with Damaris to prevent future academic problems from arising and to support her social/emotional development (American School Counselor Association, 2016). I felt Damaris could benefit from a counseling referral and decided that family therapy was necessary first in light of Damaris's primary concerns after our short-term individual counseling ended. I also made sure Damaris knew that I was a supportive person in the school to whom she could turn if her struggles became too difficult to manage. To maintain our connection and rapport, I checked in weekly with Damaris for several weeks and then tapered our check-ins to every two to four weeks. During our check-ins, I focused on ensuring that Damaris received the supports she needed and that her social/emotional concerns were not impacting her academic development or her overall well-being.

One important lesson that was reaffirmed from working with this student is that sometimes there will not be a clean resolution of the student's concern. Although Damaris's situation improved significantly from the time she was referred, I know she still had struggles in relation to questioning her sexual identity along with how much she could openly share with her family. She still felt a need to hide some aspects of herself from her family and although that was not ideal, I had to remind myself that as a school counselor working with students living in complex systems, I cannot expect the situation to be resolved completely. Damaris was no longer having difficulties participating in choir, her grades remained solid, and she reported fewer emotional breakdowns at school and at home. She also had access to more resources, and her support system grew from the time we initially started meeting. During one of our sessions, I mentioned a community organization that held support groups for students questioning their orientation, but Damaris declined, as she said that her mom would find out and that would cause more difficulties. This was another lesson learned for me, as I had not fully processed the challenges of having a student pursue community resources that would in essence "out" them before they were ready.

Finally, and I think most importantly, I learned a significant amount from this student's situation in relation to application of counseling techniques and multicultural considerations. I chose the Adlerian approach because I knew of its benefits in providing encouragement to the student while taking family, cultural, and societal issues into consideration. However, in my work with Damaris, I found I needed to teach myself more about acculturation and in this process learned about the concept of biculturalism. The Adlerian approach was adaptable for integrating biculturalism concepts into our counseling sessions and it was the first time I was able to do this with a client. I found it to be beneficial for Damaris, and it helped me expand my multicultural counseling skills in the process.

DISCUSSION QUESTIONS

1. What are the four phases of Adlerian counseling? What are techniques a school counselor could use in each phase?
2. What are the pros and cons of using the Adlerian counseling approach in a school setting?
3. How is Adlerian counseling adaptable to incorporating multicultural counseling concepts?

REFERENCES

American School Counselor Association (2016). ASCA position statement: The school counselor and LGBTQ youth. Retrieved from www.schoolcounselor.org/asca/media/asca/Position-Statements/PS_LGBTQ.pdf.

Aslinia, S. D., Rasheed, M., & Simpson, C. (2011). Individual psychology (Adlerian) applied to international collectivist cultures: Compatibility, effectiveness, and impact. *Journal for International Counselor Education, 3*, 1–12.

Baams, L., Grossman, A. H., & Russell, S. T. (2015). Minority stress and mechanisms of risk for depression and suicidal ideation among lesbian, gay, and bisexual youth. *Developmental Psychology, 51*(5), 688–96. doi: http://dx.doi.org.ezp1.lib.umn.edu/10.1037/a0038994.

Caterino, L. C., & Sullivan, A. L. (2009). Applying Adlerian therapy in the schools. In R. W. Christner & R. B. Mennuti (Eds.). *School based mental health: A practitioner's guide to comparative practices.* New York, NY: Routledge.

Croake, J. W. (1983). Adlerian parent education. *Counseling Psychologist, 11*(3), 65–71.

Hamm, J. S., Carlson, J., & Erguner-Tekinalp, B. (2016). Adlerian-based positive group counseling with emotionally troubled youth. *Journal of Individual Psychology, 72*(4), 254–72.

Nguyen, A. D., & Benet-Martínez, V. (2007). Biculturalism unpacked: Components, individual differences, measurement, and outcomes. *Social and Personality Psychology Compass, 1*, 101–14.

Nguyen, A. D., & Benet-Martínez, V. (2013). Biculturalism and adjustment: A meta-analysis. *Journal of Cross-Cultural Psychology, 44*(1), 122–59.

Rosario, M., Schrimshaw, E. W., & Hunter, J. (2009). Different patterns of sexual identity development over time: Implications for the psychological adjustment of lesbian, gay, and bisexual youths. *The Journal of Sex Research, 48*(1), 3–15.

Sommers-Flanagan, J., & Sommers-Flanagan, R. (2015). *Counseling and psychotherapy theories in context and practice: Skills, strategies, and techniques* (2nd ed.). Hoboken, NJ: Wiley.

Part III

Reality/Choice Theory

We almost always have choices, and the better the choice, the more we will be in control of our lives.

—William Glasser

With reality/choice theory, all humans have five basic psychological needs: belonging, power, love, survival, and freedom. School counselors work daily with students to help meet their needs while at school as well as outside of school. This theoretical approach allows school counselors to focus on how to help students gain understanding that they are responsible for their lives and that they can make changes to their lives. In addition, reality/choice therapy focuses on the present, considers cultural differences, and is an active therapeutic approach, which is a natural fit for school counselors. This empowerment occurs in school counseling through developmental guidance lessons, group work, as well as the individual work that is seen in the next three chapters.

While reading about the challenges presented in the next three chapters, consider how the authors navigated the needs and goals of the individual students, as well as how the counselors help their students self-discover their "control" of the situation. Each counselor builds a collaborative relationship and guides the students to develop their own plans to move forward. Finally, explore the actions that each student takes to maintain or gain control of their freedom, which is the heart of reality/choice theory and how their school counselor helps their students take responsibility for their actions.

Chapter Seven

Mia

This case study is set at Hillside Elementary School, a rural elementary school in the Midwest with slightly more than seven hundred prekindergarten through fifth grade students. Most of the students at Hillside Elementary school are Caucasian, and more than half qualify for free and reduced lunches. The school counselor is the only counselor serving the seven hundred students. This case was inspired by my time working with elementary-aged students.

As you read this case study, look for the following:

- Which clues lead the counselor to determine the likely cause of Mia's behaviors
- How the school counselor first works to establish a trusting relationship with Mia to help her open up and feel comfortable
- Ways that the school counselor accounts for the student's five basic needs: survival, love and belonging, power and control, freedom, and fun
- How the school counselor keeps conversations with Mia in the present and does not dwell on past experiences

CASE STUDY INTRODUCTION

The following case study is about Mia, a seven-year-old Caucasian student in second grade at Hillside Elementary School. Mia lives with her parents, Karen and Jack Miller, and her four-year-old sister Maddy. School assessments show that Mia is a gifted student and consistently scores in the ninety-seventh percentile and above in both reading and math.

Hillside Elementary School, which has slightly more than seven hundred students in prekindergarten through fifth grade, has about one hundred students in each grade level and twenty-five students per classroom. The student services department at Hillside consists of one school counselor, one school social worker, and a half-time school psychologist that splits his time between Hillside and the other elementary school in the district.

Karen Miller referred her daughter Mia to the school counselor for avoiding school and nail biting. Mia also struggles in large groups and being at school triggers her responses. The school counselor works with Mia and her family to develop relaxation and breathing techniques. By helping her meet her physiological needs, the school counselor is helping Mia control her own reality.

With Mia, I applied choice theory/reality therapy, which was first pioneered by Dr. William Glasser. The foundation of choice theory is a strong relationship between the counselor and patient and also ensures that the patient's five basic needs are being met in healthy ways (Glasser, 1998).

INCIDENT

On a cool mid-November day at Hillside Elementary, the school is buzzing with excitement for the upcoming holiday break. Students are walking through the hallways a little more loudly than usual and the lost-and-found table is starting to grow taller as single mittens and forgotten hats pile on top.

Yesterday morning I had a lengthy phone conversation with Mrs. Karen Miller regarding her second-grade daughter, Mia. Mrs. Miller received a truancy warning letter from the school because Mia already had missed six days of school this year and she called to share with me her concerns about Mia's absences.

Most mornings, according to Mrs. Miller, Mia wakes up just fine, but as the morning progresses, Mia starts to complain of a headache or stomachache. Her parents tried taking Mia to the doctor on a few of these occasions, but there doesn't seem to be anything medically wrong with Mia. On the days Mia does stay home from school, she always seems to feel better by the afternoon, but the symptoms return again the next morning. Mia assures her mom that she isn't being picked on at school, has a good group of friends, and likes her teacher, but Mrs. Miller isn't sure what to do at this point to help her daughter get to school every day.

I asked if Mrs. Miller had any other concerns about Mia, and she said that the only other concern was that Mia bites her nails frequently at school and even at large family gatherings, and she often comes home from school with her cuticles bleeding and her nails bitten down to nubs. Mrs. Miller sounds like she has tried everything she can think of to get Mia to come to school. She said she would be happy for me to work with Mia and would help in any way she could at home.

The headaches and stomachaches sounded like somatization, in which psychological concerns manifest as physical symptoms. This is not uncommon in a school setting. The school nurse often refers students to me whom she sees in the office on a consistent basis complaining of stomach- and headaches, because the causes of their symptoms are sometimes psychological and not physical, especially when it happens frequently or at a certain time of day. Before meeting with Mia, I wanted to talk with her teacher and learn more about how she is doing once she gets to school.

After school I met with Mia's teacher, Mr. John Garfield, who is a tall man in his early thirties with wildly curly red hair and a warm smile. John has been teaching at Hillside for the last five years and is a favorite of students and teachers alike, and he had lots of great things to say about Mia. He reported that Mia does very well academically and is a high achiever. Although Mia seems shy and doesn't raise her hand in class, when Mr. Garfield meets with her one-on-one, she always understands the material and does well on assessments, though she takes a long time to finish her work. Mr. Garfield suspects that Mia wants all of her work and answers to be perfect.

During free time, Mia can often be found in the library corner of the classroom reading a book or playing a game with a friend or two. Mia has friends in class and is kind to all students, but she does seem uneasy when the class gets a little too talkative or does large group activities. John said he really didn't have any big concerns about Mia, but he did notice that she has missed a fair amount of school. It seemed to me that Mia was not feeling safe in large groups at school and was afraid of making mistakes academically. Perfectionism is common among gifted students like Mia, and I wanted to find ways to help her feel safe in school and in her classroom.

Although the information from Mrs. Miller and Mr. Garfield was helpful, I still didn't have any definitive answers and knew I would need to meet with Mia to learn more. Unfortunately, I didn't really know Mia apart from seeing her and the rest of her classmates in bimonthly classroom guidance lessons, and hearing from Mr. Garfield that she was shy would require some relationship building before we could dig in to any real issues. Mr. Garfield said that 10:00 am during silent reading time would be an ideal time for me to meet with Mia.

Lucky for me, Mia was in school the following day and arrived at my room precisely at 10:00 am with a pink hall pass in hand. Mia was wearing a black Hogwarts t-shirt and gray leggings and had her long brown hair swept back into a neat ponytail. She smiled meekly and knocked on my door, even though it was open.

"Hi, Mia! Thank you so much for coming to see me this morning. Come on in and have a seat," I said warmly and gestured toward the table and chairs in the corner.

Mia complied and quietly sat down.

"Mia, I am so glad to get to talk with you today! Since we don't know each other very well yet, I was wondering if we could get to know each other a little bit today. Do you like to play games?"

"Yes," Mia replied, with just a hint of a smile.

"Why don't you go over to my shelf and pick out one that you like?" I asked, gesturing to a bookshelf in the corner of my office that held stacks of card games and board games.

Mia spent a minute or two carefully looking over the games as though this was a big decision and she didn't want to choose incorrectly. She finally settled on Uno and brought it back over to the circular table.

As I dealt the cards I asked, "Mia, could you tell me a little bit about the people who live at your house?" I hoped to pull Mia out of her shell and help her feel comfortable opening up to me.

"Well," Mia began in a voice so soft I had to lean in to hear, "I live with my mom and dad and little sister Maddy. And my dog Freddy."

"What kind of dog is Freddy?"

"He's a golden retriever," Mia replied with a little bit of a smile.

"Oh, golden retrievers are one of my favorite kinds of dogs!" I said enthusiastically after noticing her smile. "What are some things that you like to do with Freddy?"

"He sleeps on my bed and lays by my feet when I do homework or read, and my mom said that I am strong enough now to hold his leash when we walk him." By now I could see a little bit of Mia's protective shell cracking away. Building relationships with students is a necessary part of school counseling, and I wouldn't be able to help Mia without first building a relationship with her. She was talking a little bit louder and with a lot more excitement than she had been just a few moments ago.

"Freddy sounds like a great friend. Do you have any good friends here at school?" I asked, attempting to shift the focus from home to school.

"Yes, I have Anna in my class, but my best friend is Ellie and she is in Mrs. Hallstad's class this year," Mia said sadly. I chose not to ask more about Ellie right now but made a mental note that not having Ellie as a safety net in her class this year could be part of what was keeping Mia from feeling safe in second grade.

"How do you like Mr. Garfield's class this year?" I asked.

"Well, I like Mr. Garfield a lot. He is funny and we do a lot of fun stuff in class."

"Is there anything you don't like?"

"Some of the boys are really chatty and kind of loud, and I don't really like that." I also filed this fact away for later, thinking that the combination of not having her best friend in class along with some loud classmates might be contributing to Mia's lack of feeling psychologically safe in class and at school.

"It seems like you have been sick a lot this year," I noted.

"Yeah, I have been getting a lot of stomachaches and headaches," Mia answered.

"That's not good. Why do you think you have been feeling so sick this year?"

"I don't know." When students tell me they "don't know" the answer, they often just do not want to say, but if given a little more time and a safe environment, they will usually offer an answer. Mia seemed like a deep thinker, and I guessed that she probably did know why she was sick so often. In fact, I would bet she thought about it quite a lot.

"If you had to guess, why do you think you have been sick so often?"

"My mom said it was because I don't want to go to school. But I do want to do well in school. I want to go to college someday," Mia said, sounding conflicted.

"That's great that you want to do well in school and go to college. Mr. Garfield said that you work very hard in class and are a very focused learner." I try to avoid telling students that they are smart, especially gifted students like Mia. When students feel like they are expected to be smart, evidence to the contrary such as getting a question wrong when called on in class can damage their self-image. Instead, I focus on actions that students can choose, such as working hard or focusing on their learning.

"Well, I did okay last year, but second grade is much harder and I don't think I am doing very well." I was surprised to hear Mia say this, since her teacher and her test scores said the opposite of what Mia was telling me.

"What makes you think you aren't doing well?" I challenged.

"I don't know. When Mr. Garfield asks me a question in class, sometimes I forget the answer."

I was starting to put the pieces of Mia's puzzle together. She freezes in class when the teacher unexpectedly calls on her, starts to feel sick in the mornings, avoids school and large groups, and is worried that she is not going to achieve her mental picture of success, which includes doing well in school and going to college. In classroom guidance lessons we have been talking about having a growth mind-set and how our brain learns, so I decide to explain to Mia how her brain is functioning in these situations.

"Do you want to hear about how amazing our brains are?" I ask.

"Sure," Mia answers enthusiastically.

"We can think of our brain in two main parts. The first part is the part of our brain that we share with animals like Freddy," I say, making a fist with my left hand. "This part helps to keep us alive and can help us stay safe by making us respond fast when we think we are in danger. When we think we are in danger we can run away from the danger, fight the danger, or freeze so we can't be seen. Can you think of a time when it would be really helpful to fight, get away, or freeze really fast?"

"Like if a mean animal was chasing us?" Mia guessed.

"Yes! That would be a great time to react fast so we could stay safe. The animal part helps our heart beat faster so we can get blood to our legs to run away, and our breathing might get faster to get more oxygen flowing, and we might stop digesting our food because our body needs to focus all of its energy on staying safe. We also have a thinking part of our brain that goes over the animal brain," I say, placing my right hand over and around my left fist. "This is the part that lets us think logically, tell a joke, or solve a story problem in math class. When we are in danger, the thinking part stops working so the animal part can take over.

"Sometimes though, when we are not in danger, the animal part of our brain mistakenly believes we are and reacts. This can be a problem because then we can't use the thinking part of our brain to solve the problem, and it can also make our heads or stomachs hurt because our bodies are getting ready to fight, run away, or freeze. Does that make sense?"

"I think so. I think my animal brain is taking over sometimes." I believed that Mia's animal brain was taking over when Mr. Garfield called on her in class and when she got up to get ready for school in the morning. Her body was trying to keep Mia safe from the perceived threat of school and was causing her physical problems.

"The good thing is that you can learn to be in control and get your thinking brain working again. Would you like to learn how?"

"Yes!" Mia answered excitedly. I decided to teach her breathing techniques, which would allow her to meet her physiological needs and feel calm and safe. Helping Mia gain control of her body also could help her meet her psychological need for power and control.

"Great. Now that the weather is getting colder, do you have a favorite warm drink that you like to enjoy?"

"Hot chocolate with lots of marshmallows." Mia was now very animated and talking in a voice that was easy to hear.

"I like hot chocolate, too, but sometimes it is too hot to drink right away. I want you to imagine you are holding a mug of hot chocolate in your hands," I said. Mia and I both put our hands out and held our imaginary mugs.

"First, we are going to smell the hot chocolate," I said, lifting my imaginary cup up and taking a slow breath in through my nose. Mia did the same.

"Great. Now when we breathe out, we need to blow off our hot chocolate to cool it down, so breathe out slowly through your mouth. If you breathe too fast, you might blow out one of your marshmallows," I cautioned jokingly. Mia laughed and blew on her mug. "Let's take a few more breaths like this, smelling our hot chocolate, then slowly blowing on it to cool it down." As we breathe, I could visibly see Mia relaxing, lowering her shoulders and sitting back in her chair.

"And that's all there is to it. When we take a few slow breaths in through our nose and out through our mouth, we are telling our animal brain that the danger has passed and we can go back to using our thinking brain. Do you think you could try this when you get worried in class or in the morning before you come to school?"

"I think so. It seems really easy."

"It gets easier when you practice," I said, handing Mia a scratch-and-sniff hot chocolate sticker from my sticker drawer. "I want you to practice your deep hot chocolate breathing tonight at home and tomorrow morning, and this sticker will help you remember. Do you think I should call and let your mom know about the hot chocolate breathing so she can help and practice too?" I asked, knowing that when parents can help support at home what I am doing at school, students improve a lot faster.

"Yes!" Mia responded quickly. "I don't think my mom knows about the animal and thinking brains, either. Can I teach her about that tonight?"

"You can definitely teach you mom about the animal and thinking brains," I reply. "And maybe your dad and your sister, too!"

Mia smiled and I walked her back to her room. Before we entered her classroom, she put the sticker in her backpack and I told her we would meet again tomorrow to learn another way to help get back to the thinking brain. I wanted to give her lots of tools in her toolbox that she could use when she started to feel worried.

Mia showed up right on time for school the following day, excited to tell me how it went teaching her family all about their animal and thinking brains. We worked to identify places in her body that hold on to her worry, which for Mia was her stomach and forehead. By learning to relax the muscles in her stomach and forehead through guided relaxation, she complained of fewer stomachaches and headaches. I followed up with Mia's mom that afternoon and let her know that Mia was excited to share what she learned with her family tonight. The next week, I called to see how Mrs. Miller thought Mia was doing. Mrs. Miller said that they had been doing the hot chocolate breathing and guided relaxation techniques together at home before bed and in the morning before getting ready for school. Although there were still a few times that Mia had a headache or stomachache, it was much better than before.

After I appraised him about Mia's anxiety, Mr. Garfield worked out a system with Mia in which he would tug his ear a few seconds before he called on her in class so she could take a deep breath and be ready with her answer. I talked with Mr. Garfield about our goal to make sure Mia's physiological and psychological needs were being met, and he worked to make the classroom environment a safer place, which he happily reported was beneficial for other students as well. He offered all students more choice in their assignments and seating, made sure his classroom procedures and routines were consistent, and conducted morning classroom meetings to build a safe environment among the students. He also met with Mia individually to ensure she was being challenged in class and was not bored.

CASE DISCUSSION

I decided to use reality therapy to help Mia, which is based on choice theory and was developed by William Glasser in 1965. Reality therapy works particularly well in the school setting because it focuses on finding solutions to current issues and concerns that the student can control instead of focusing on the past or factors outside of their control. Choice theory contends that we choose our behaviors, consciously or unconsciously, to meet our basic physiological and psychological needs. The five basic needs are survival, love and belonging, power and control, freedom, and fun. Because our behavior always represents our best choice at that time, in order to change behavior, we must either change what we want, change what we are doing or how we are coping, or change both what we want and what we are doing (Glasser, 1998). When working with Mia, I helped her to understand her physiological need for her animal brain to feel safe and to change the way she was coping with this need by teaching her breathing and relaxation techniques. In collaboration with Mr. Garfield, we also helped to support Mia's needs through classroom practices that benefited all students. Providing teachers with suggestions for effective classroom management is encouraged in the American School Counselor Association (ASCA) national model and is an effective way for school counselors to partner with teachers to support all students.

Choice theory works well with a variety of situations in a school setting. In his article "Giving Students What They Need," Erwin (2003) describes how understanding students' five basic needs and applying them to the classroom fosters an engaging learning environment in which students are internally motivated. Erwin also reminds us that all students are motivated, though they might be motivated to act in ways that are different from what is expected by their teachers. When we see a student who is not following school rules or who seems unmotivated to learn, we can assess which of the student's needs are not being met in a way that allows him or her to flourish in school. Using the tenets of choice theory, we can use the foundation of a positive relationship with students and build ways to appropriately meet students' needs in order to help all students engage more fully in the school setting. In his article "'Choice Theory' and Student Success," Glasser (1997) describes how he applied his theory at an at-risk school and saw dramatic successes among the students. All teachers and staff were trained in Glasser's "quality school" concepts, which focused on meeting students' basic needs, and over time, the school saw improved test scores, reductions in discipline problems, and students who were motivated to learn.

As in Mia's case, choice theory can be used to meet the unique needs of gifted and talented students in the school setting. Robertson (1999) explains that gifted and talented students often focus on achievement or the need for power while neglecting their need for fun, freedom, or belonging. We might see this in students who work on academics all of the time instead of participating in sports or recess or who feel different from their peers and have few friends. In some schools and settings, gifted students might find themselves bored and unchallenged, which Glasser (1986) contends is the opposite of fun. Robertson (1999) presents a program consisting of five lessons to help teach gifted students to balance their needs and make sure all needs are being met, which could work well with all students. Teachers and school counselors must look at each student individually and assess which needs are being met appropriately and which needs remain unmet or inadequately met in order to help students find and maintain balance.

Choice theory was originally called "control theory," since it informs us that we can only control our own behavior; we cannot control the behavior of others (Glasser, 1997). School counselors regularly address situations in which students feel like others made them act in a certain way and can work with students to help them see the power and control that they have over their choices and behaviors. However, as Wubbolding (2015) reminds us, we do not have full control over our behaviors, and we react without thinking. This is especially true for children who are still developing and learning how to interact with the world. Counselors using reality therapy avoid blaming the student for their choices and instead work with them to meet their needs in a different way through a different choice the next time.

One of the common limitations in a school like Hillside Elementary is the large number of students being served by just one school counselor. The American School Counselor Association (ASCA) recommends one school counselor for every 250 students, though most schools do not meet that standard. If the school counselor had a smaller caseload, perhaps the counselor already would have developed a trusting therapeutic relationship with Mia and even may have been able to intervene earlier, before Mia's school avoidance and anxiety symptoms became severe. The ASCA model encourages all school counselors to provide counseling to students who are absent or tardy, like Mia. The earlier school attendance issues can be addressed, the better the outcomes for students. With the help of her school counselor, Mia was able to find better ways to meet her needs, which allowed her to attend and engage in school and learn strategies that will help her in second grade and beyond.

DISCUSSION QUESTIONS

1. What physiological and psychological needs was Mia meeting through her nail biting and school avoidance?
2. Why did the counselor teach Mia about how her brain works? Do you think it was an effective and appropriate strategy?
3. In what other situations might it be appropriate to use choice theory/reality therapy in a school setting?
4. Give some examples of how teachers and school counselors can meet the five basic needs of students in schools. How can teachers and school counselors ensure that their own five basic needs are met?
5. What are some of the unique needs that school counselors should be aware of when working with gifted students like Mia?

REFERENCES

Erwin, J. (2003, September). Giving students what they need. *Educational Leadership, 19*–23.

Glasser, W. (1986). *Control theory in the classroom.* New York: Harper & Row.

Glasser, W. (1997, November). "Choice theory" and student success. *Education Digest, 63*(3), 16–21.

Glasser, W. (1998). *Choice theory.* New York: HarperCollins.

Robertson, J. B. (1999, January/February). Helping gifted/talented students improve their balancing acts. *Gifted Child Today Magazine, 22*(1), 34–37.

Wubbolding, R. (2015, July). The voice of William Glasser: Accessing the continuing evolution of reality therapy. *Journal of Mental Health Counseling, 37*(3), 189–205.

Chapter Eight

Tina

The school counselor in this case study works in a large metropolitan area on the mid-Atlantic seaboard in a suburban school district with about fifty-five hundred students and has been a school counselor there for fifteen years. The population is predominantly white, with a growing minority population of about 20 percent. There are evident divisions in socioeconomic status within the school district. There are two other counselors in the middle school. The counselor has a "home base" in reality therapy/choice theory but believes it is necessary sometimes to draw from other approaches and to know when to revise or borrow from other counseling theories for the benefit of the child. She is also sensitive to the role that trauma or adverse childhood experiences may play in school behavior and whether students have successfully integrated those experiences. Although she appreciates eclecticism, she does not want a hodgepodge theoretical approach. She views her role as helping children to develop both academic and social success. The following case study focuses on the use of reality therapy/choice theory.

As you read this case study, look for the following:

- Triggers for the undesirable behaviors and adults' responses to them
- Instances of blaming and issues of responsibility
- Small successes that materialize into more sustained success (either validated by the school counselor in the case study or not)
- The language of choice theory as the case study progresses
- Hints regarding the use of a medical model

CASE STUDY INTRODUCTION

Tina, an eleven-year-old, sixth-grade girl, attended a sixth through eighth grade suburban middle school with more than nine hundred students and a school counselor ratio of approximately 325:1. The administration in the middle school consists of the principal and assistant principal. The middle school mirrored the diversity of the broader school district. Often, groups of students clearly were defined by socioeconomic status, and it was challenging for students to move from one group to another. This middle school used a team-teaching approach and had weekly "team" periods for clubs and recess activities.

Tina struggled with classroom focus, self-control, completing class assignments, and maintaining friendships. Although she was an attractive and often pleasant child, she sometimes became angry and physical with other students. She had verbal and crying outbursts when she believed she was being wronged or did not get her way. She liked to tell other students what to do. She enjoyed helping in the classroom and was usually the first to offer her assistance to the teacher, thriving on the attention. However, offering to help at inappropriate times or when no help was required became an avoidance behavior. Sometimes she walked around the classroom when she was supposed to be doing individual work and talked to other students, usually to avoid a task or just to get involved in their business. At other times, she refused to move from place to place in the classroom or school hallways. These behaviors became increasingly disruptive to her own and others' educational progress. There came a point in which she walked out of the classroom when angry. She consequently had numerous disciplinary office reports and was removed from riding the bus to school. She lived with her biological mother and stepfather, two older half-siblings, and a younger sibling. Tina is white and says her two older half-siblings are mixed race. Her biological father died when she was a toddler and she maintained that she had no recollection of him. She was at least of average intelligence and enjoyed physical activities and sports but never played on any organized teams. She loved art, reading, and writing, despite little support and resources at home.

INCIDENT

Tina was referred for school counseling by her team of teachers to help her improve classroom focus and complete class and homework assignments, as well as to learn social skills and coping skills for when she became angry. Lately, her grades were dropping, homework was not being turned in, and her focus on classwork had been decreasing, evidenced by her avoidance of work in class (e.g., walking around the room instead of doing her individual work, doing "dance moves," asking to go to the bathroom, talking to other groups instead of working in her own group, getting off-topic during group work, and disparaging those in her group.) On several recent occasions, she left the classroom without permission, presenting safety and security issues. Thus, her anger and avoidance behaviors were escalating. Her mother was supportive of the referral but had little investment in the process.

Rapport was easily established in the first counseling meeting, as it was apparent that Tina enjoyed the attention. Although this can be beneficial for beginning the school counseling relationship, promoting independence and behavioral change can be a challenge when the attention appears to be so craved. Also, because I taught regular classroom guidance lessons, I had the start of a relationship with her. Initially, she was verbal, talking incessantly, so I had the opportunity to listen with warmth and understanding, establishing the first step in reality therapy: creating a supportive relationship that would eventually lead her to become a responsible person of strong self-worth. I knew that I needed to show Tina that I genuinely cared about her so that I eventually could ask her what she really wanted, an important initial step in reality therapy. I then gave her the choice of standing to play a "question ball-toss" game (using a ball with various topics and questions printed on it) or sitting in a beanbag chair to talk, and she chose the ball-toss game. It was apparent that she enjoyed the movement and the challenge of the game. She was of average build and was dressed in athletic shorts, a bright-colored shirt, and white, soiled sneakers. I checked for accuracy of what I observed, mentioning, "It seems like you like games, both indoors and outdoors?" She agreed and offered, "Oh, yes. But I don't go to any sports or anything. I just play at home and at lunch recess." It was helpful for me to get to know her likes and dislikes, including subjects of interest and family and friends, through this type of interview game. I learned that she liked soccer, dancing, cheerleading, art, and almost every subject in school. I then could begin to help her to develop important aspects of reality therapy: a "success identity" and an awareness of what behaviors were "working" and "not working" for her.

However, when asked what she thought she could "get better at in school," she answered that she thought she was "doing pretty good with everything in school." I knew this was not an accurate assessment; for a moment, I wanted to get out her current grade sheet and missing homework assignments to show her, but in keeping with reality therapy, I encouraged Tina to evaluate her own behaviors and whether they were productive in getting what she really wanted. I would not want to appear to be leveling criticism, since the counselor as well as the client need to avoid this in reality therapy. The idea is instead to learn to be responsible by making and accepting one's best choice at a given time, rather than becoming too self-critical or dwelling on the past. Focusing on current behavior, I asked her to tell me more about what she thought she was "doing pretty good with," and she answered, "language arts and special subjects, like art and gym." This type of self-evaluation is a tenet of reality therapy. I validated this part of her assessment. Then we were able to go over her current grades and assignments together. I asked her what she thought it meant to be a "student." She answered, "to come to school, do homework, and learn," affirming that she wanted to do those things.

I suggested we construct a T-chart of what behaviors of a student looked like. I used this method as a teaching tool, since part of reality therapy is teaching skills needed for success (Glasser, 1984). She asked if she could add decorations to the chart and I agreed—acknowledging her willingness to create the chart and use her artistic talents to make it look visually pleasing— as long as we stayed focused on the chart. In the language of choice theory, I let Tina know that I was there to help her and that we could work on ideas for the chart together. We came up with student behaviors such as listening to directions, following the directions, looking at the teacher or speaker, doing homework on time, coming to school, trying your best, remaining quiet when someone else is speaking and not interrupting, writing, or typing on the computer, cooperating in a group, calming down when mad, and so forth. Tina then could pinpoint areas that she currently thought she was "good at" and acknowledge the areas she could improve upon, such as "not talking during class," "getting classwork done," and "completing homework and bringing it to school." I was able to say to her, "So, talking in class, interrupting others, and having incomplete work and homework is not working for you?" She agreed with this self-assessment and realized that those behaviors were not "working for her" if she really wanted to do well in school and have friends.

An asset for Tina was her good attendance; she rarely missed school. I noticed this in her records and pointed it out to her. She said that she liked coming to school. I asked her, "What makes you want to come to school?" She answered, "I like most of my teachers and doing cool projects—you know, learning new things." I now had additional confirmation of what she wanted. This led to an action plan—an essential part of reality therapy—to complete her classwork when it was given and to do her homework and bring it back to school. In order to accomplish the classwork, Tina referred to the general student behaviors on her T-chart and decided what she would need to do to make that happen. She acknowledged that she would need to talk to others less if she was doing individual work; to stay in her space to complete her work, no leaving the classroom; to listen to and follow directions; and to try first on her own and then ask for help from the teacher if she needed it so that she could keep her frustration from becoming an angry outburst. She was aware of deep breathing exercises from a classroom guidance lesson and decided that was something she had control over and could incorporate into her action plan. She also made a commitment to do her homework during her study hall and at home after dinner. We made an appointment the following week and then for weekly check-ins.

The next week saw only a slight improvement in Tina's schoolwork and behavior. Tina had not left the classroom without permission, but the teachers reported that she still wandered inside the classroom and talked to others at inappropriate times, though less frequently. She had one outburst when a teacher told her that she had to sit down and get to work or she would have to go to the office. Although I was able to validate some success with parts of the plan, I could not allow Tina to make excuses for not accomplishing other parts of the plan, consistent with reality therapy. For instance, she complained that she could not do her work because she didn't "get" the directions; another girl "kept staring at her" so she "had to tell her to knock it off"; and she was not turning in homework because her little brother was "bugging" her.

I could see that we needed to rework the plan. I spoke with the teachers about Tina's desire to learn as well as her need for attention from adults as well as peers. I suggested checking with Tina to ensure she understood the assignment directions and to approach her without argument if she was off-task, using choice theory language such as, "I'm not going to argue with you. I'd like you to focus on your task, but I am here to help you if you run into a problem." These steps also would help to avoid punishment, such as being sent to the office, which would be inconsistent with reality therapy.

I then asked Tina what she thought happened with the plan. She wasn't quite sure, but she didn't like "being stared at." I noticed that Tina needed help not to dwell on this, since a tenet of reality therapy is not to "dwell on the past" and previous mistakes. We reviewed the plan and practiced the desired in-class behaviors. I asked her what she could do if someone was looking at her while she was trying to work and she shrugged. I asked her if what she was doing in class was working for her. She thought some things were, such as facing the teacher when she was speaking and thinking in her head that she "can do it." Now, how could I help her shift her perception that the girl "staring at her" was preventing her from completing her work? This is an important aspect of reality therapy, that a person controls only one's own behavior and that change comes only from the person taking responsibility, not external controls.

I stated, "So you're angry that the girl staring at you is making you not do your work." Tina replied, "well, sort of." I asked her if she could control what the girl looks at. Tina said no. I asked, "What could you do if this happens again, since you can't control what that girl looks at?" Tina paused and said, "I guess I could just ignore it—forget about it and focus on finishing my work." "So you could look away and ignore it. You could 'focus and finish'?" Tina said, "Yes. How about if I make a little sign that says, 'focus and finish'?" I said, "Sure—like a little reminder on an index card?" Tina said enthusiastically, "Yes! Can I decorate it with gel pens?" That phrase became her mantra for taking control of a situation. (Although I saw the need for development of more successful social skills, since other alternatives besides "ignoring" could be used, I did not want to incorporate too much at once into her plan. She had taken responsibility to come up with a workable problem-solving solution on her own. A small group for friendship skills and support would be beneficial in the future.)

I decided to move on to the problem of homework. When I asked, "Do you want to get your homework done on time?" she grew angry and said her little brother followed her around all night and wouldn't let her do her homework. Although I affirmed her frustration with her younger brother's behavior, I thought about the need for eliminating excuses and blame in reality therapy. I asked, "What could help you get your homework done?" This veered into a conversation about her family life and ultimately a solution that involved Tina talking with her mother and trying to find a different quiet spot in the house.

I continued my work with Tina throughout most of the school year, checking in weekly for four weeks, then twice per month or less, always attempting to demonstrate to her that I believed in her ability to make changes, to find healthy alternative solutions to problems, and to grow her strengths. During other sessions, we used the T-chart method to understand the characteristics of a friend and to develop a plan to have more friends. She wanted to make booklets about school, friends, and family. Utilizing her creativity, sometimes she used a small composition notebook, blank sheets of paper, or a book creator computer program. The booklets became not only stories of her life and goals, but problem-solving models. She came up with phrases to remind her of her accomplishments and of what she had control over. Achieving both academic and social success was essential to developing her self-worth. Tina would need skills on both fronts as she progressed through middle school.

Strategies and techniques used during school counseling sessions included revising plans and positive goal setting (Charney, 2001) and bookmaking creations through writing and drawing as well as the use of computer programs that built on her visual and language arts skills. A behavioral reminder "school skills card" (e.g., "focus and finish" reminder), calendar to keep in her binder, a booklet of calming strategies to which she could refer that included a self-regulation scale for anger management, breathing techniques including mindfulness, and physical exercise were also utilized.

Tina also participated in a small group for friendship and social skills (O'Rourke and Worzbyt, 1996) in which skills were taught and practiced (e.g., empathy/perspective taking, conversation skills including talking-and-listening and waiting, conflict resolution ideas including learning to stop and think, "Will this help or hurt?" asking/inviting, giving compliments, etc.). In the group, I facilitated and modeled positive affirmations to note Tina's strengths and to encourage this type of language among group members. The group was also beneficial to Tina because she often had conflicts with peers both in and outside of the classroom that stemmed from her desire to "do things her way" or her excessive talking and interrupting. She found it diffi- cult to take responsibility for her words and actions, but this improved with the reality therapy approach as she began to realize the things that she could change and what was out of her immediate control. For instance, when friends refused to play the game that Tina wanted to play at recess, Tina responded by crying, yelling, and sometimes remaining on the playground for ten to twenty minutes after recess ended. She learned how to respond as a "problem solver"—to stop and think about her choices. She had a "bank" of ways to solve this type of situation (e.g., ask to join another game already in progress, go elsewhere and do another enjoyable activity either alone or with a different person, etc.). This was a difficult change for Tina to make, as she was used to reacting quickly with anger and she did not have models of this type of problem solving at home. With practice, the tantrum-like behavior diminished toward the end of the small group sessions.

Although Tina had a desire to do better in school, she often brought up her relationships in school and with family and friends as our meetings progressed. She usually spoke negatively about her siblings and the difficul- ties in getting along with them. She talked in a matter-of-fact way about the death of her father and occasionally spoke of her stepfather. She seemed to have a positive view of her mother, noting that her mother worked hard at her restaurant job, even though she complained about her boss. In school, she developed a good relationship with several teachers. They noticed her enthu- siasm for learning as well as her desire to be helpful and wanted. As a school counselor, it was also necessary for me to build a good relationship with her teachers in order to facilitate Tina's academic and social improvement. I could see the need for Tina to develop confidence in her ability to handle problems and disappointments effectively, as well as in academics. It would continue to be important for Tina to recognize her strengths and utilize them positively to build success; as her school counselor, I needed to look for opportunities in school to encourage this development and even to help to create those opportunities. My involvement as school counselor included frequent teacher consultations, as well as developing a teacher check-in plan regarding classwork and homework, assisting teachers in accommodating Tina when she needed to take a break or to move around (without leaving the classroom), and supporting the teacher's classroom management. All of this became part of a "toolkit" to help Tina become more successful in and out of the classroom. Tina's language arts skills were average to above average, but a short-term program of math intervention was put into place to boost those skills and her confidence, in addition to her success identity and self-worth. In addition to in-school supports, I met with Tina's mother and secured community resources to meet some of the family's needs.

During sixth grade, Tina built on the abovementioned strategies and began using a calendar to increase her attention to school responsibilities. Since she had made strides in learning simple breathing techniques and gained confidence in using her words to avoid peer conflicts, she recognized that reacting physically was not working for her. She then was able to ride the school bus again. Toward the middle of sixth grade, more homework was given, and during the second half of the school year, Tina turned in her homework 90 percent of the time. Her office discipline referrals decreased; during the last two months of sixth grade, she did not have any office discipline referrals. In assessing her progress, she could name coping strategies and social problem-solving skills and usually took responsibility for completing and turning in homework. As the school year progressed, she had fewer classroom outbursts and no longer left the classroom without permission. Her skills grew, and she still sought school counseling, but on a less frequent basis.

Tina felt proud to be recognized at the end of sixth grade with a certificate from the assistant principal when she volunteered to help with a community environmental project in which she had used her artistic strengths to create a poster. She was gaining positive outcomes for her actions and using more effective coping strategies. Tina continued to seek out school counseling for peer difficulties but was better able to accept responsibility for her part in a conflict. One day, out of the blue, she proudly brought a photo to show me of herself as a baby with her mother and biological father. I commented that the photo seemed special to her and she seemed happy to have it. She agreed and said she wanted to create a book about "some things her mother told her about her father." Tina said she was hoping her mother would sign her up for dance or soccer outside of school. She still had little support at home and would continue to need validation and encouragement in order be successful in school.

CASE DISCUSSION

This case demonstrates the need for a variety of creative techniques within the realm of reality therapy/choice theory to develop and build the child's strengths to promote self-worth and autonomy. I realized the importance of developing a warm, caring counseling relationship, the main theoretical approach of reality therapy/choice theory, as well as teacher consultation and coordination of school and community resources. Working with Tina periodically during the course of the school year allowed time during her preadolescent development to utilize her strong verbal skills and build upon her interest in learning and her openness to new social problem-solving skills. At this age, Tina still had a thirst for knowledge and was open to adult help. Through the reality therapy approach, I could address the need for her to become more self-sufficient and take responsibility for her words and actions. A little gem of a book, *The Language of Choice Theory* (Glasser and Glasser, 1999) influenced my counseling approach. The language of choice theory was useful with teachers and with Tina, as it allows for understanding but always comes back to self-control and responsibility. In the school setting, Tina was able to see her successes and receive immediate feedback.

Tina learned about taking responsibility for herself and her choices, even though she could slip into blaming and wishing that she could "make people do what she wanted." The reality therapy approach showed her how to make a plan of action to solve problems and to fix things that were not working for her (Glasser, 1965). This approach essentially gives a person permission for trial and error, which is how strength and success is built. An outgrowth is a sense of confidence that "I'm okay even though I made a mistake and can find different ways of doing things that work." The approach allows people to build on small successes, and this is important for our students. Reality therapy allows for mistakes and revisions and a positive outlook that a person always can make changes in behavior. The teaching aspect of reality therapy is also appealing and practical (Glasser, 1984). So many skills for effective living can be taught creatively. I also gave much thought to Glasser's departure from an "illness" perspective and rejection of the medical model, which is sometimes difficult to square with a culture that is basically the opposite. (This is not to diminish the real need for medicine and proper medical treatment, but an important aspect to note in reality therapy.)

With limited support at home, I believed that school always would be important to Tina's academic, social, and personal success. Reality therapy/choice therapy with its emphasis on strength building, self-responsibility, and the development of realistic goals in a plan of action, seemed to fit naturally with what Tina needed. Tina did take pride in her school accomplishments as she began to see successes. I also thought that Tina's own communication with her mother had improved, helping her deal with her little brother's interruptions and learning more about her deceased father.

As a professional school counselor, I appreciate the guidance that the ASCA national model provides. I like the simplicity of being able to break down school counseling into the three domains—academic, social-personal, and career—then delving into the specific objectives of each area. When I am thinking about the counseling approach I am employing, I'm also considering the implementation of the ASCA model standards. These were the standards I was working toward with this case:

Academic Development
1.1 Improve Academic Self-Concept:
    1.1.01 Articulate feelings of competence and confidence as a learner
    1.1.02 Identify attitudes and behaviors that lead to successful learning
1.3 Achieve School Success:
    1.3.01 Take responsibility for actions
Career Development
2.2 Develop Employment Readiness:
    2.2.01 Develop a positive attitude toward work and learning
Personal/Social Development
3.1 Acquire Self-Knowledge:
    3.1.01 Develop positive attitudes toward self as a unique and worthy person
3.2 Acquire Interpersonal Skills:
    3.2.05 Use effective communication skills
3.3 Self-Knowledge Application:
    3.3.01 Use decision-making and problem-solving model
    3.3.04 Develop effective coping skills for dealing with problems

As I reflect on this case, I became more convinced than ever in the importance of continuously projecting an attitude of "never giving up," or in reality therapy terms, "refuse to give up" (Glasser, 1965) to the student not only in the counseling setting, but at other times as well. It is easy to become discouraged when students are not progressing as quickly as I or the teachers would like. I needed to persevere in finding even the smallest positive step toward change and to reflect that back to the child. I have become more adept at this and find this counseling skill so powerful in helping students recognize that they are capable of setting positive goals and making behavioral changes. I learned a lot about advocating for the student by listening to students, developing relationships with them, and building on strengths. As a school counselor in touch with many students, teachers, and administrators, I also believe I have a leadership role in working toward the development of a positive, caring school climate that encourages self-responsibility and problem solving (Glasser, 1969). I realize that this is an ongoing task that requires many hands. In this case, it was difficult to get support from the child's family, and as a school counselor, I felt limited in my ability to assist Tina with her home environment. I hoped that Tina would use the skills she had been taught both in and out of school.

I see reality therapy/choice theory as a conduit of hope. It is the belief that people can learn to accept responsibility for their choices and make positive changes, learning from mistakes but moving quickly forward, and that children can learn successful skills for life through a supportive counseling relationship in a respectful, caring school. This is just what our students need so desperately today.

DISCUSSION QUESTIONS

1. What are the benefits of using reality therapy/choice theory in the school setting?
2. Overall, what are the limitations of reality therapy/choice theory?
3. Should Tina's home life have been more thoroughly explored, including the impact of the death of her biological father at a young age?
4. What other skills could have been part of the "teaching phase" of the reality therapy approach in this case?

REFERENCES

Charney, R. S. (2001). *Teaching children to care: Management in the responsive classroom.* Greenfield, MA: Northeast Foundation for Children.

Glasser, W. (1965). *Reality therapy: A new approach to psychiatry.* New York, NY: Harper & Row.

Glasser, W. (1969). *Schools without failure.* New York: Harper & Row.

Glasser, W. (1984). Take effective control of your life. In Corey, G. (1986). *Theory and practice of counseling and psychotherapy.* Monterey, CA: Brooks/Cole Publishing.

Glasser, W., & Glasser, C. (1999). *The language of choice theory.* New York, NY: HarperPerennial.

O'Rourke, K., & Worzbyt, J. (1996). *Support groups for children.* New York, NY: Brunner-Routledge.

Chapter Nine

Harvey

The case below follows a first-year school counselor as she builds and develops a relationship that utilizes techniques in reality therapy with Harvey, a high school student, as he struggles for academic achievement and autonomy.

As you read this case study, look for the following:

- How individuals from Harvey's school and community typically resolve conflict
- The significance of retaliation to Harvey and his community members
- Neighborhood conflicts that predate the school counselor, staff members, and Harvey
- How Harvey's methods of maintaining autonomy, safety, and achievement for both him and his brother conflict with each other and cause challenges
- Why Harvey mistrusts school staff and how that impacts the counseling relationship

CASE STUDY INTRODUCTION

This particular school counselor works in a large urban school serving students from seventh through twelfth grades that is 99 percent black/African American. The racial demographics of school faculty is 85 percent Caucasian and 15 percent black/African American. Twenty-three percent of the students receive special education services and 87 percent of all students score below basic on reading and math state standardized testing. The school counselor to student ratio is 1:800, which is well over the American School Counseling

Association's recommendation of a 1:250 ratio (American School Counseling Association, 2012).

The school counselor works at a school that serves students from a large area on the north side of the city that consists of many different neighborhoods. Historically, this school has been on the state's persistently dangerous schools list as a result of the constant serious incidents. The school counselor finds out from the assistant principal that these serious incidents are a result of "decades" of neighborhood conflict that spills over into the school.

INCIDENT

It was not easy accepting the fights and other confrontations as simply a "reality of this school." And being a first-year school counselor who had never lived in the city where I now worked made it even more difficult for me to normalize. Where I went to school, physical altercations were few and far between. Here, the opposite. Fights and arguments are the go-to problem-solving solutions for our students. It can be exhausting. The thought that my role could impact what appeared to be a long-practiced culture filled me with nervousness and uncertainty, but also the opportunity to make positive change. Getting to this point would require developing relationships with the student body, my colleagues, and the community of which I was now a part.

It was the beginning of the school year and faculty and staff had their first professional development meeting. The focus of the meeting—and the focus for the school year—was making improvements to the school's student behavior issues. With additional funding from the school district, the goal was to create and implement a plan to decrease suspensions and expulsions, increase attendance, and create a better school climate to reinforce positive student outcomes and ultimately to remove the school from the state's "persistently dangerous schools" list. I decided to pose a question to the group: "Why do our students fight so much? Could it be bullying or something else?" Our assistant principal, Mr. Liles, told the group that the school had been this way for as long as he could remember and explained that many of the fights in school were a result of "decades" of neighborhood conflict that spilled over into the school. Even though our school served students from one large area on the north side of the city, that area consisted of many different neighborhoods, some of which have "beef" (or conflict) with each other. Our school was basically a meeting ground for all of these different neighborhoods that disliked each other. Now it made sense. I dwelled on the possibilities and challenges for some time.

It was the second week of school and Harvey was sitting in my office. Silent. I had seen him before in the hall and hanging outside after school on the steps. He was a tenth-grade student and fairly ordinary, maybe slightly eccentric. In a seventh through twelfth grade school of more than eight hundred, Harvey was the type of student who easily could fall under the radar. The students who often fell under the radar were the ones whose needs were not always as visible as the students who stood out due to either disciplinary action or high academic achievement. And now here Harvey was, sitting in my office. Scratches and bruises, with an unhappy face. What was I to do? It was Tuesday, the first day back to school after a three-day weekend when he was escorted into my office by Mr. Liles first thing that morning during breakfast. He said that Harvey could benefit from speaking to me and instructed Harvey to tell me what happened on Friday. "I already told you that I'm good and I'm gonna be good," Harvey told Mr. Liles, looking at the floor. Mr. Liles shared with me that on Friday, Harvey was jumped by three boys in the bathroom and beaten badly. Apparently the boys were not identified yet and Harvey was not giving much more information. Harvey looked visibly distressed. His school uniform was disheveled and sloppy, his tie loose, and his pants wrinkled.

Mr. Liles left. I said, "It sounds like Friday must have been pretty rough for you, Harvey. How are you today?"

"It was but I'm good now." Harvey rubbed his face with his hands and yawned.

"Did you get to do something you enjoy or get a chance to relax over the weekend?" I already could tell based on Harvey's lack of a response to Mr. Liles that he did not really want to talk about what happened Friday, at least for right now. It was early in the morning and I had a feeling that he also did not want to be in school right now, so I decided against confronting him about the incident.

"Actually the opposite. My mom worked all weekend so I had to take care of my brother the entire time so I got to sleep really, really late."

I thought to myself his discomfort in being here may be due to tiredness. "Well, did you at least get an opportunity to eat breakfast this morning?"

Harvey shook his head no. I wasn't surprised that after staying up late the night before and potentially oversleeping this morning, there was no time to eat. Luckily there was still time to get breakfast before his classes started.

"There's still time for breakfast. Would you like to go eat something first?" Harvey shook his head yes, thanked me, and left my office.

When Harvey returned, his face looked a little brighter, his tie was fixed, his shirt was tucked in, and he had a full breakfast tray in his hands. "Mr. Liles said I could get my breakfast and come back in here and eat. Is that okay?"

"I was beginning to think you weren't going to come back. Of course it's okay."

"At first I wasn't going to, but I'm tired and didn't really want to be bothered with anyone."

"I can understand that, Harvey. Especially after you seemed to have such a long weekend."

Harvey munched on his sausage link. There was no modesty in how he was eating. It was clear that he was hungry. He then paused for a second and began to slow his eating. Almost like he came to a revelation.

"After this, do I have to go to class?"

"Well, Harvey, I don't know what Mr. Liles said, but I'm certainly not keeping you here if you don't want to be here. You can go back to class if you want to, or you can stay here for a little bit and talk with me for a while longer."

Harvey began to pace his food consumption. I took note of this and concluded that Harvey was not ready to see his peers or potentially the boys who attacked him (and were not caught) yet. He could have been afraid, angry, or still processing all that happened.

"Okay. But I'm not a snitch, just so you know. So don't waste your time if that's why I'm here." I was a bit shocked by his sudden change in tone and unprovoked hostility. He was still angry about Friday and rightfully so. I could imagine that Mr. Liles had been badgering Harvey about giving up the names of his attackers. Perhaps he was saying this to me because he couldn't differentiate the assistant principal and school counselor's role in his issue.

"Harvey, as your school counselor, my role is to support you and your needs. If you don't want to share the identities of those boys to me, that is fine. My responsibility is to your well-being right now."

Harvey seemed less tense now. I could tell that this was a sensitive matter to him. I had to make sure he guided where this conversation went. Utilizing my basic listening skills, I said, "I don't know all the details about what happened Friday, but it seems like you're still upset about what happened. Am I right to think that?"

"I'm furious about what happened. What makes it worse is that I didn't even do anything to them, and they snuck up on me, so I couldn't even really defend myself. But I'm good now."

"It sounds like a really scary situation, to be minding your own business and for something like that to happen so unexpectedly."

"It happens to a lot of people."

I believed Harvey when he said it happens to a lot of people. What I did not believe was that he was "good." After an unprovoked attack by three people and a weekend with little opportunity to decompress and relax, even the most resilient of students would find being "good" a challenge. I felt that Harvey was downplaying the effect of this traumatic event to appear strong and in control. However, I was happy that he was talking to me more.

After a brief pause before I could say anything else, Harvey continued, "I think it was these dudes that live on the north side that did it. There are people in my neighborhood that are beefing with them and they probably knew that I was from the south side and attacked me just for sport." He then gave more specific information and told me that although all the students technically live on the north side of the city, residents still identify themselves as living on the north side, south side, and so forth within that section. Harvey explained that the north side and south side had conflicts since before his mother was a child. For Harvey, it was the culture he was used to.

"So you're faced with the threat of violence simply because of where you live?"

"Yup," Harvey said matter-of-factly. "It just is what it is. But the worst me or my brother got was maybe a few dirty looks or threatening words. Never anything physical before Friday."

"You have a brother? Does he go to this school as well?"

"Yup. He just went to eighth grade. He's real smart and is in a lot of afterschool activities to stay away from our neighborhood. I don't want him to go to this school during high school. He can probably go to a college prep school or maybe even a private school. I *have* to make sure he's good and doesn't get involved in any of this."

"You care very deeply about not only your brother's safety, but also his success as well. It sounds like something you really want for him."

Harvey nodded, almost excitedly. "What part of the city are you from?" he asked, turning the spotlight on me. It was a question I was not expecting from Harvey at that moment. I could tell that he was trying to find something we could connect with. Of course I wanted Harvey to trust me and to feel like I would understand anything he told me, but I knew it was important to be transparent with him. Although we may be of the same ethnicity, the environment I grew up in was very different than his.

"I'm from outside the city. It's a lot different there. Smaller and a lot quieter. This might be the largest school I've ever been to."

"I already figured you weren't. I just wanted to see if you would answer." It felt like Harvey was testing me. Seeing if I was being genuine.

He continued, "I like small and quiet. If I go to college, it's going to be in a small town where everyone knows each other." I noticed Harvey's choice of words: using "if" instead of "when" when talking about college. This is something I wanted to explore later. Still, I could tell that he was really beginning to open up. It hadn't been that long ago this morning when he wouldn't even look at me.

An integral part of implementing reality therapy is that the school counselor must value the client-therapist relationship and must work with the client to develop a relationship that involves trust, acceptance, and understanding. In this case the student–school counselor relationship. Before closing out our first session, I told Harvey that although he told me several times that he was "good," I was naturally still concerned for his safety during the school day and that not identifying his attackers was not going to ensure his safety.

Harvey said, "Well, being a snitch and telling Mr. Liles won't ensure my safety, either. Sure, it might offer me some protection in school, but you all aren't there when I'm walking to and from school with my brother or when I'm in my neighborhood. I gotta handle this the right way." Harvey left on that comment. I could not help but feel how unfortunate it was that Harvey did not trust the school staff to protect him. I also thought this whole ordeal was not quite over and pondered over Harvey's statement that he would handle the issue the "right" way. What was the "right" way—and was it truly "right" at all?

Sometime after Harvey left my office, I expressed my concern about Harvey's safety in school with Mr. Liles. He then told me that Harvey's three attackers had been identified from the hallway cameras on the fifth floor that morning. They were suspended for five days and sent home with their parents. I was relieved by the fact that Harvey would be safe in school for at least today but still wondered if "handling the issue the right way" would be a possibility now that his attackers had been reprimanded. I was looking forward to following up with him.

Later that week, Harvey returned to my office and immediately made himself comfortable. "So I heard about what happened to those dudes," he said. I stated, "Yes, they were caught on camera right before they attacked you and afterward. How do you feel about how things played out?"

"It still makes me look like a snitch to everyone. Besides, they'll be back next week and I have to make sure that I handle this the right way so they know that a suspension doesn't make up for what they did."

"Could you tell me a little bit about what exactly the 'right way' is, Harvey?"

"I have to do to them the same thing that they did to me. That makes it a fair trade." I was shocked by how much Harvey was sharing on just our second visit. "I notice that you said 'I *have to*' several times. How come you 'have to'?"

"I have to because my mom and cousins and people in my neighborhood already know what happened. I didn't even get a chance to tell them before people here from school did. If I don't do anything, then I'll be a punk, and they might continue after me and maybe even my brother. I gotta show them that I'm not a chump. That *we're* not chumps." From what Harvey said, it sounded like he was under pressure (both real and perceived) to prove himself to his attackers and to his community that he was strong, and if he did not, he, his family, and his community would suffer for it.

"Harvey, I can tell that your loved ones mean a lot to you. You feel like you need to protect the safety and reputation of yourself and your loved ones through retaliation that is equal to what your attackers did to you."

"I have to. It is what it is. I want me and my friends to be ready for them when they come back to school. That is the plan," Harvey had told me.

Harvey would retaliate because he felt like he had to, but is what he *has* to do the same as what he *wants* to do? "Harvey, it sounds like the pressure to do something to these boys is coming from outside forces. Is this right?"

"What do you mean?"

"Meaning that your peers, family, and community members want you to do something about this. But what about what you want to happen? Just you, no one else." Harvey paused and looked at me like I had suddenly stopped speaking English. It was becoming clear to me that throughout his thinking process about how to resolve this conflict, he was acting as an extension of his community on the south side, not necessarily as an individual.

"I just want to forget about what happened and continue doing what I was doing before this all happened. I just want to go to class, take care of my little brother, play basketball, wrestle, do normal teenager stuff. That's what I want."

"So retaliating is not what you want. It's what you feel like you need to do to go on living your life the way it was before this all happened?"

"Yup."

It appeared as if there was a disconnect between what Harvey wanted and how he gets what he wants. Harvey thought that by attacking those boys, his life would return to the way it was before Friday, but how much had Harvey thought about the potential consequences and outcomes of attacking? My goal was to help Harvey align his plans with what he wanted. I created a worksheet that illustrated the WDEP (wants, doing, evaluation, and planning) system (Wubbolding, 2011), which is an essential component to reality therapy. It allows the student and counselor to map out what the client wants (W), what they are doing now to get what they want and how it makes them think or feel (D), to evaluate the "doing" process and how it contributes to or hurts what the student wants (E), and then to create realistic and attainable plans and goals to change behavior and generate outcomes that align with the student's "wants" (P). It seemed that all pieces of the WDEP system would benefit Harvey in this conflict, especially the evaluation part. "Harvey, I have a worksheet here that I want us to work on. It will help you articulate and map out what you want for yourself and how your actions, decision making, and plans contribute to what you want. Is that something you are interested in trying with me?"

"Yeah, I guess."

"So, Harvey, could you tell me a little bit more about what you want through this conflict."

"Well, I just want to be able to come to school every day safely and leave safely. My brother, too. I want my attendance to be better so I can do better in my math and science classes. If I keep my grades and attendance up, I'll be eligible to try out for the basketball and wrestling teams next month. I don't ask for a lot."

I wrote down on the worksheet his three main wants and showed it to him. "Is this correct? Safety for you and your brother, better attendance and math and science grades, and the opportunity to try out for basketball and wrestling."

"Yup, that's really it. That's it and I'd be happy."

Harvey had clearly expressed what he wanted through all this. I concluded that my role was to help Harvey identify the potential outcomes of his proposal to retaliate against his attackers and see if those possibilities would help him get those "wants" that he identified earlier. If those possible outcomes did not align with his "wants," Harvey needed to develop and implement a new realistic plan. After finishing the "doing" and "evaluation" process of the WDEP system, Harvey concluded that retaliating could result in two plausible outcomes. One outcome could be that Harvey gets caught by police or school officials and then suspended or even arrested. The other outcome could be that he does not get caught but the other boys may then try and retaliate against Harvey or even his brother, perpetuating this cycle of violence that existed in the school and community. Harvey said, "if I do retaliate, I'll either lose time in school, which impacts my 'wants' of better attendance, grades, and tryouts, or my brother might be in danger, which is the other 'want' I talked about." Through this self-evaluation process, Harvey was able to figure out that what he planned to do would not get him what he wanted. The next step was to replace what he was doing with a new plan.

"Harvey, how are you feeling now after you have come to this conclusion?"

"I don't know. On one hand, I'm happy that I was able to think this out before I actually carried out my plan, but on the other, I'm not sure what to do now."

"That's understandable, Harvey. You seem like you're a bit conflicted about what your next steps will be." Through this entire process, I wanted Harvey to not only make a decision that would support the results he wanted, but also to understand that the type of outcome that he gets is based on the choices that he makes. Although it is true that the unfortunate events that led Harvey to my office were out of his control, it was important that Harvey knew that maintaining happiness, or his "quality world," were in his control.

Harvey's next step was to find a plan that would better align with his wants that was also realistic and attainable. Some of the goals Harvey and I set were seeking out afterschool tutoring sessions to improve his performance in math and science. This plan was achievable because it was offered by the school and would give Harvey something constructive to do while waiting for his brother's afterschool activities to end. Another goal was trying to get at least eight hours of sleep every night and to eat breakfast. Small, yet achievable goals could help Harvey reach his "wants" more effectively than retaliation. My role as Harvey's school counselor was to hold him accountable to the goals that we set through weekly check-ins. However, concern for his safely and possible trauma from the attack left me feeling unsettled as his counselor. This was something I would monitor in future meetings with Harvey.

CASE DISCUSSION

I know that as a school counselor using reality therapy to work with my students, I must first work with each student to build a strong, positive relationship in order to achieve therapeutic outcomes. I need to be able to possess personal qualities of "warmth, sincerity, congruence, understanding, acceptance, concern, openness, respect for the student, and the willingness to be challenged by others" (Corey, 2017). These qualities allow the student to trust me, and I can then gain a deeper understanding of the underlying conflict or issue that the student is experiencing. It is important for students to understand that they have choices and they can consider their full range of options before making a decision.

Choice theory is "the underlying theoretical basis for reality therapy" (Mason & Duba, 2009) and recognizes that all humans are motivated by needs: survival, love and belonging, power of achievement, freedom or independence, and fun. Choice theory recognizes that all individuals "store information inside our minds and build a file of wants called our Quality World" (Corey, 2017). The "quality world" fulfills the needs of the individual, and in order for therapeutic outcomes to take place, the school counselor must fit into the student's quality world. Through choice theory, I recognize that students make their choices based on what was the best attempt to satisfy their needs. Although I admit that I am not from a community like Harvey's, I must understand and take into consideration Harvey's worldview and need to retaliate against his attackers to prove his strength and protect his family. The solution of putting matters into someone else's hands (school police, assistant principal, or even mine) were not acceptable to Harvey. It is important that I am able to align myself with the needs of my students and understand their obligations to adhere to school district policies.

The goal of using reality therapy is to help students realize that they are responsible for their own happiness and lives. Using reality therapy, I work with students to help them take personal responsibility, evaluate their choices, and assist them in planning for any changes. In order for me to be successful using reality therapy, I must consider two aspects of my approach: the counseling environment and the questioning process (Stupart, 2018). The counseling environment refers to getting to know students and what their wants are, to stay focused on the issue at hand, to promote responsibility, to ensure that students are getting what they want, and to never give up on the belief and expectation that change is possible. The questioning process refers to four questions regarding what the student wants, what the student is doing, how the student is evaluating his or her choices, and what the student is planning to do.

To ensure a quality counseling environment so that reality therapy can be successful, I must take time to build relationships with my students. Relationships with students are not built in a day, so I must remain diligent and continue to work to get to know them and to build trust between us. For example, in the case of Harvey, I used my ability to be genuine and empathetic with Harvey to allow him to trust my sincerity and open up to me. Building a relationship with Harvey allowed me to explore what Harvey's wants and needs were. We came to understand that Harvey wanted himself and his brother to be able to go to school and leave school safely each day. Harvey also shared that he wanted to improve his attendance so that he could do better in his math and science classes, which in turn would enable him to try out for the basketball and wrestling teams.

When using reality therapy, I must help the student stay focused on the issue at hand. By remaining focused, I promote responsibility within the student and can help to ensure that the student's wants are being met. Finally, the last component of the counseling environment for reality therapy is for me to instill perseverance in the student. I must hold the belief that change is possible.

The questioning process for reality therapy allows me to better understand and explore with the student what the student's wants are and what the student has been doing to satisfy those wants. Questions that I ask the students follow a WDEP approach: what they want, what they are doing, how they are evaluating their choices, and what their future plans are. Examples of questions a school counselor can use include:

1. Wants (What do you want?)

     a. How do you want your life to be?
     b. What kind of student do you want to be?
     c. What kind of relationships do you want?

2. Doing (What are you doing?)

     a. How are you feeling?
     b. What choices are you making?

3. Evaluate (Is it helping?)

     a. Is what you are doing helping you get what you want?

4. Plan (What else can you do?)

    a. How can you move into action?

    b. How can you find a more effective way to get what you want?

Reality therapy and choice theory have several applications to the American School Counselor Association (ASCA) national model. I recognize my ethical obligation to provide all students with the necessary counseling and psychoeducational services while at the same time being aware of the school policies for addressing the situation. I must also take into account the ASCA Mindsets & Behaviors for Student Success (ASCA, 2014). In this case study, I considered behavior standards B-SMS 1: demonstrate ability to assume responsibility; B-SMS 7: demonstrate effective coping skills when faced with a problem; and B-SS 5: demonstrate ethical decision making and social responsibility (ASCA, 2014). Using reality therapy and choice theory is also a method I can use for response services since reality therapy and choice theory are designed to address and meet students' immediate concerns and needs.

Regarding the ASCA national model's call for comprehensive school counseling programs, counselors are able to "value and respond to the diversity and individual differences in our societies and communities" (ASCA, 2014) using reality therapy and choice theory. The WDEP method allows me to address the individual needs and wants of each student. This method also allows me to teach students to advocate and set goals for themselves so that they can learn to promote their own academic and personal achievement. Understanding the needs and wants of students, I also can work with members of the educational team to use their "skills of leadership, advocacy, and collaboration to promote systemic change as appropriate" (ASCA, 2014).

DISCUSSION QUESTIONS

1. How can the school counselor address Harvey's concerns about returning to school if he does not feel safe in this environment anymore?
2. As the only secondary school counselor in the school, how much support can the school counselor provide Harvey? As a first-year counselor, how can the counselor use the ASCA national model to promote positive outcomes for all students involved?
3. How does the school counselor build community in the school to prevent altercations in the community in the future?

4. What is the role of the school counselor in establishing positive relationships outside of school with community members who historically have had conflict?
5. How might the school counselor's values or beliefs align with or oppose the decisions made by the student?
6. What are the limitations of reality therapy?

REFERENCES

American School Counselor Association. (2012). The ASCA national model: A framework for school counseling programs (3rd ed.). Alexandria, VA: Author.
American School Counselor Association. (2014). Mindsets and behaviors for student success: K–12 college- and career-readiness standards for every student. Alexandria, VA: Author.
Corey, G. (2017). *Theory and practice of counseling and psychotherapy* (10th ed.). Belmont, CA: Thomson Brooks/Cole.
Mason, C. P., and Duba, J. D. (2009). Using reality therapy in schools: Its potential impact on the effectiveness of the ASCA national model. *International Journal of Reality Therapy, 29*(2), 5–12.
Stupart, Y. (2018). How to promote teen school engagement with reality therapy. *Owlcation.* Retrieved from https://owlcation.com/academia/UsingRealityTherapytoPromoteTeenSchoolAchievemen.
Wubbolding, R. (2011). *Reality therapy.* Washington, DC: American Psychological Association.

Part IV

Family Systems Theory

That which is created in a relationship can be fixed in a relationship.
—Murray Bowen

Family systems theory was included in part IV of this book, since school counselors work with not only their students, but also the students' families. There are five interlocking concepts with family systems theory: differentiation of self, triangulation, multigenerational emotional processes, emotional cutoff, and societal emotional processes. These concepts are processed to move past "blaming" in families to then explore the roles of each family member. School counselors accomplish this by coaching their students to explore the dynamics of their family and the interdependent relationships within the family. Throughout the next three chapters, school counselors also work with families in the school setting when it is necessary to help the student.

As you read, explore how the school counselor navigates advocating for the student as well as collaborating with the student's family. There is a need for trust between not only the counselor and student, but also among the family and the school community. Each school counselor strives to build this rapport and trust with the student and his or her family, even when the family is not present. This ripple of effect causes the counselor to differentiate his or her counseling approaches and challenges the school counselor to meet the needs of all involved.

Chapter Ten

Abigail

High-stress counseling situations require that school counselors react thoughtfully and purposefully. A depth of knowledge and experience is helpful but not always available to them. Developing a response plan and then implementing it during a crisis requires that they respond to factors and considerations that cannot be predicted. The goal of this chapter is to provide a case study for practicing school counselors and school counselors in training to explore the use of family system theory as they work with clients in high-stress, real-life situations. The scenario described is a compilation of actual incidents. The elementary school is located in a large rural area in the upper Midwest. With four hundred students, kindergarten through fifth grade, the majority of the students self-identify as white (98 percent), as do staff and administration.

As you read this case study, look for the following:

- Consider the process involved: this case involves many others beyond the student, such as the parents, and outside resources are affected
- Consider the ripple effect: the case seems straightforward; however, the numerous layers and impact are great
- Take time to reflect on how you would react and respond effectively.

CASE STUDY INTRODUCTION

Abigail, a fourth grader in a rural school of four hundred students, has just participated in the final developmental guidance lesson on "good touch" and "bad touch." These developmental lessons, an important prevention component of the American School Counselor Association (ASCA) model at the elementary level, include encouraging children to tell an adult if they are ever

117

in a situation in which they feel uncomfortable. Building student support and resiliency through self-reporting is a vital component of this classroom guidance lesson. As the school counselor, I coordinate classroom lessons like this one as an integral part of our school's prevention plan. Of course, prior to implementing these lessons, I met with the building principal, the school counseling district team, and fourth grade teachers to review the lessons and potential outcomes. We also discussed how this self-reporting connected to our overall crisis plan. This type of preparation and planning help to connect potential scenarios and responses when we encourage students to self-report potential harmful situations.

INCIDENT

A week after the presentations, I received a written note in my school counselor mailbox, a locked mailbox that sat outside the school counseling office door. The note read, "My father has been touching my sister and me in bad ways." The student signed her name, Abigail, to the note.

As a school counselor, this is a moment you want to be ready for, a situation in which a student is calling on your professional skills in a specific way. You want to be prepared for just such a scenario to help you to help the student receive the support and follow through that he or she will need. Unfortunately, when I read that note, I momentarily went blank. The planning and preparation escaped me. But we, as school counselors, need to respond.

The preparation for what "might be" had turned into an actual, high-stress, student crisis. In reviewing our school response later, there were many moments when we struggled to determine the next step. We needed to consider the ethical and legal expectations, the short- and long-term impact on Abigail and her sister, Florence, as well as the rest of the family.

My initial meeting with Abigail was straightforward and honest. "My father has been touching me in bad ways [using the language of the classroom lesson]. I want this to stop and I am worried about my younger sister."

She had clearly thought about what she wanted to do, and the classroom lesson opened the door for her to let someone know. She discussed the issue regarding her father freely. It was important to ask open-ended questions and let Abigail talk. Through letting her share what was happening at home, she was empowered. By using open-ended questions, I allowed her to talk about what was happening. "My father has been coming into my room at night and I wasn't sure what to think about what he was doing. I just knew I didn't like it."

"You did the right thing by giving me a note and talking with me about this, Abigail. As we have talked about before, there are some things that I don't keep confidential, and this is one of them. I need to make some calls so that you and your sister are safe."

"Okay," said Abigail, "I want this to stop." She showed little hesitation, even when reminded that reporting would involve other community professionals to ensure she and her sister were safe. It was clear that she understood what was happening, that the interaction was not healthy or appropriate between her father, her, and her sister. As a mandated reporter, the call to local human services and/or law enforcement is a clear and required first step to keep both girls safe. Florence, the younger sister, was less prepared to discuss this issue but had talked with Abigail and knew that I had been informed. She said little and left it to Abigail to talk about what was occurring.

In subsequent meetings, both with Abigail and with the crisis team, the focus was on supporting Abigail and Florence through the tumult of the ensuing events. In the next few days after our initial meeting, Abigail and Florence both met with county social workers. In one instance they came to the school to talk with the girls. School personnel were concerned and curious. Abigail's teacher approached me in the hall, saying, "I noticed that since Abigail met with you she has been more distracted, plus I saw the social worker in the school the other day. Is there anything I can be doing to support her?" Other teachers and school personnel were focused on the details of what might be going on. One staff member asked me what I knew about Abigail and Florence's parents because she had heard that the girls were in protective custody. Not only was I dealing with the students and their family system, but I was also dealing with the school system now that the two systems had collided.

When the story of their father's arrest became public, I met with Abigail and Florence separately and focused on how they might respond to their peers. On the playground, in the halls, on the bus, and in class, both Abigail and Florence encountered students, teachers, and staff who were empathetic, supportive, inquisitive, and intrusive. The community system, school system, and family system had intersected. The crisis team, in conjunction with the school administrators, were prepared for this and had drafted statements to share. A week or so later Abigail stopped by my office. She was resolute in her focus. "Things at my house are pretty messed up right now. My dad is gone, but I am not sure what is happening. My mom and friends are supportive, and Florence seems to be happier. Everyone in town seems to know, but I just keep doing what I can, even when I feel really bad." Abigail's statement encompassed the complexity of family systems. However, when working with Abigail and Florence, it was vital to understand their world view.

Abigail and Florence separately focused on how they might respond to their peers who recognized their family in a story that appeared in the newspaper detailing her father's arrest.

CASE DISCUSSION

There are two issues in play in this scenario. The most obvious is our role as mandated reporters, which requires that we contact local human services and/ or law enforcement, relying upon school district policy and procedures and local and state laws. The focus of this chapter is on how family systems are influenced by abrupt change and how family system theory guides our work, especially during such times.

Family systems theory focuses on the structure of a family and the processes utilized by the family. Bowen (1978) suggested that the identity of individual family members emerges as part of a larger family system. He postulated that individuals from families with high levels of togetherness were more likely to struggle with individual differentiation from the family leading to increased anxiety and other psychological issues. In this example, Abigail and her family were enmeshed in relationships that are not only unhealthy, but also deter differentiation from her family.

Minuchin's (1974) structural family system model described families as organisms evolving through developmental stages, each stage bringing with it fresh demands and accommodations. Goldenberg and Goldenberg (2000) characterized the structural model as brief, direct, concrete, action-oriented interventions, which in effect change the structure of the family. Minuchin (1974) characterized behavior within the family as action and reaction mingled with family stories that form constructs that then become the present shared reality of the family.

Structural family theory focuses on the wholeness of the family system, the influence of the family's hierarchical organization, and the interrelatedness of the family subsystems on the wellness of the individuals (Goldenberg & Goldenberg, 2000). The theory also recognizes the vital role homeostasis, or the maintenance of equilibrium in the face of internal and external stressors, plays.

One key to family system theory is interrelatedness or the interrelationship among family members and their environment. Abigail's self-report affected not only her and her younger sister, but also her parents, and possibly other family members. In this instance, it is possible that family members could view Abigail as a source of harm for disrupting the family's current interrelationships, even though she was not causing the harm and the current system she described was unhealthy and potentially pointed to illegal behavior if the claims were upheld. The ensuing consequences also could be blamed on Abigail. As a result, Abigail could struggle with inner conflict caused by reporting the harm as well as the disruption of the homeostasis of her family system.

This dilemma is certainly well beyond what a fourth grader should have to deal with. However, it is important to remember that, from a system theory perspective, counselors face the conundrum of wanting to support student safety and provide emotional counseling and support to students while recognizing our own interrelatedness and role in this system. I faced a dilemma: telling Abigail she'd done the right thing by coming forward while counseling her as she navigated the resulting issues and formed her own conclusions.

Family hierarchy also plays a vital role in family systems (Minuchin, 1974). Sexual abuse is focused on power and control. Sexually abused children can be coerced into keeping family secrets with the threat that discovery will alter the family or create other negative consequences. Abigail's need to protect herself and her sister Florence intersected directly with established parental authority. Whitechurch and Constantine (1993) described hierarchy as the arrangement of layers or echelons in a family. These echelons are related to power, with parents occupying the higher echelons and children the lower. Although we may not have information on the hierarchical makeup of a family, there is potential for any member of a family to be aware of the sexual abuse but feel powerless to bring it to a stop. In this case Abigail's resolve to engage her entire family system, especially in the face of her status in the hierarchy, requires recognition and support.

Research shows that family systems can change. Whitechurch and Constatine (1993) stated that change occurs on two levels, but always as a system. Although the system embraces and understands change, forces within the system oftentimes struggle to return the system to a level of stasis. Therefore, family behavior can be examined by members' influence on each other, the interconnectedness of the multiple systems, and the interface between systems and the environment. Intergenerational boundaries, usually the relationship between parent and child subsystems, are of particular interest to system theorists.

CASE DISCUSSION

The focus of Abigail and Florence's sexual abuse case is initially legal. Family system theory helps us to consider what happens after our legal and ethical obligations are met. Understanding Abigail's family system and its reaction to patterns helps us to support Abigail, Florence, and their family. It also allows us a pathway to understand how family systems shift away from individual cause and effect yet are influenced and affected by other systems, including schools and courts. Abigail not only changed her life, but influenced the wholeness, hierarchy, and interrelatedness of her current family system. The interlocking of family with larger systems, described as "suprasystems" (Minuchin, 1974) allows for and demands deeper understanding and thought when dealing with individual clients. A move toward recovery is the next step. That approach can be multifaceted and there are several theories available to use. We strive as counselors to know our students; also knowing the families can help in our daily practice. Using the family systems theory in looking at this case allows us to consider factors that could help build resiliency and bring healing for this student.

It is also good to reflect and review on all crisis situations. Reporting abuse links to crisis interventions and planning for the clients, school, families, and community. It is vital that we, as counselors, know and practice, the mandatory reporting procedures for our school and district. Not only being prepared, but also looking at how you continue to build success for the students you work with is key. Ultimately, letting Abigail know that what she did was brave and encouraging her on the road to healing was the next step in the process of recovery.

DISCUSSION QUESTIONS

1. How might family systems theory be utilized when working in a high-stress counseling situation?
2. How does family systems theory combine with your school policies?
3. How might family systems theory be utilized when debriefing and following up with school and outside resources to ensure that best practices were followed?

REFERENCES

Bowen, M. (1978). *Family therapy in clinical practice*. New York, NY: Jason Aronson.
Goldenberg, I., & Goldenberg, H. (2000). Family therapy. In R. Corsini & D. Wedding (Eds.). *Current psychotherapies* (6th ed., pp. 375–406). Itasca, IL: Peacock Publishers.
Minuchin, S. (1974). *Families and family therapy*. Cambridge, MA: Harvard University Press.
Whitechurch, G., & Constatine, L. (1993). Systems theory. In P. Boss, W. Doherty, R. LaRossa, W. Schumm, & S. Steinments (Eds.). *Sourcebook of family theories and methods: A contextual approach* (pp. 325–52). New York, NY: Plenum Press.

Chapter Eleven

Tia

This case involves a middle school counselor about midway through her second year in the profession. She had previous experience working across all levels of schools while completing internships in her graduate program and discovered a true passion for working with students at the middle school level. The work there was exciting, nonstop, student focused, and centered in the personal/social domain of school counseling. It didn't take long before she found her home away from home in the large, diverse, suburban middle school where this case takes place. It was at this school that she began her career straight out of graduate school and hoped to establish herself.

Today, this counselor subscribes to local and national professional school counseling groups in order to stay as current as possible on professional development opportunities, changes in the field, and legislation affecting school counselors in the region. It is through this work and these experiences that she can continue to establish herself in this demanding profession.

The school in this case serves a population of roughly 1,000 students across three grade levels, leaving each counselor with a caseload of about 330 students. The school is unique in the level of support staff, as the ratio of counselors to students is much closer to the ASCA national model's recommendation of 1:250 than many similar schools across the region. This is a direct reflection of the values of the administration, who have made it clear that they invest in support staff and the important work they do. The school is also unique when compared to others in the region in that it is highly diverse (the community includes families with a variety of racial, ethnic, and religious backgrounds), has about a 40 percent free and reduced lunch population, and offers a variety of learning opportunities and supports for students (including response-to-intervention classes, a gifted and talented program, and an immersion program). The school's students face the challenges that many students across the region face: sexual abuse, homelessness, mental health disabilities, incarceration of caregivers, substance use and addiction, pressure at home, and racism, just to name a few.

As you read this case study, look for the following:

- The unique background of the student prior to enrollment
- The dynamics of the relationship between the parents and child
- The family's level of trust and willingness to share information with staff at school, especially concerning the student's past
- The nature of the student's presenting concerns and possible root causes
- The application of family systems theory in the case and specific techniques used by the school counselor

CASE STUDY INTRODUCTION

Tia, an eighth-grade, African American thirteen-year-old student (who looked closer to seventeen), first walked into my life as a midyear transfer. This is not so uncommon at my large, busy, suburban-but-feels-urban middle school where it sometimes seems as if the front doors are revolving; students come and go all year long. Some leave only to return a few months later. Some disappear into what seems like thin air until we later come to learn that they moved out of state over the summer. It soon became clear, though, that for three main reasons, Tia was not like every other student who passed through those revolving doors. First, I learned through my secretary's registration email that Tia was coming to us straight from a residential care and treatment facility out of state. I would later learn that Tia spent a few months at Conrad Academy, a dialectical behavior therapy (DBT) residential program where she and about a dozen other adolescents ate, slept, participated in intensive DBT, and received an education in a fully supervised, locked-down facility. Second, Tia had a long history of what her previous school counselor described as "bizarre" behaviors that included wearing one high heel and one flat shoe during the entire school day without saying a word about it to anyone and regularly wandering the hallways during class seemingly confused before mysteriously disappearing from that school altogether. Third, Tia's family wanted us to know as little of her past as possible. Her dad sent Tia out of state to live with her mom for the first time and to attend our school for what they hoped would be a "fresh start." They would not sign a permission form for Conrad to release any nonacademic information about Tia to us when she transferred, though later we received recommendations from Conrad that Tia should "continue with a small, general education setting where teachers can give her constant support in the classroom." This description did not match any of our general education classes, which max out at thirty-two students in our school of about one thousand students. Just like that, before we even met, I prepared myself to be spending a lot of extra time with Tia.

THE INCIDENT

When Tia and her mother first arrived, my first thought was *oh my, she looks older than I do.* Tia stood at about my height and had clearly hit puberty years earlier; she truly did look older than me. I also remember in that moment briefly recalling a discussion from my graduate school classes about how girls who develop significantly earlier than their female peers are often at higher risk for social issues, risky behavior, and other undesired outcomes.

Counselor: Hi, Tia. It's so nice to meet you. How are you today?

Tia: Fine.

Counselor: Are you ready to come back and get started?

Tia: (Barely audible) mhhm.

I showed Tia and her mom back to our conference room where I, one of our social workers, and the head of our district special education department would work together on unpacking Tia's complicated school history and gauging the best educational plan to provide Tia with the best possible start. We first discussed the differences in academic rigor, classroom time, classroom size, and staffing at our school compared to Conrad (where she received no homework, participated in only four classes, and spent much of her day in intensive therapy). Tia picked up on our concerns.

Tia: I don't want no special classes; I can handle it.

Counselor: Tia, we hear your concerns and know that you'd like to take on each of these eight classes. But we wonder if it might be helpful to get you started with seven classes and one study class where you can continue to build your academic skills and have time to work on homework.

I could see that Tia's mom was coming around to this suggestion, probably thinking about the vast changes that had been introduced in Tia's life in the last few months: exiting Conrad, moving to a different state with a different parent whom she had barely communicated with in the last year, and beginning a new school mid-term.

Tia's mom: Yes, let's do that.

Tia: No, I don't want no special classes.

Tia's mom: Well, I'm the mom here, so I'm putting my foot down.

Tia: "The mom"? You don't even know me.

It became clear at this moment that working effectively with Tia would also require Mom's support. I felt in this moment that these complicated family dynamics and baggage would have to be considered in my approach with Tia over the next year if we were to make any progress. Family systems theory seemed to be the best approach.

On Tia's first day, I paired her with another student from the same lunch period who could walk her to each of her classes for the first few days.

Tia: I don't need this girl to show me around. I know where everything is already.

When she said those words, I was taken back to registration day when I began to show Tia and her mom around the school. Tia said the same thing, that she already knew where everything was. I played along and said that it was more for Tia's mom, though I was curious to test Tia's claims. As I suspected, as we toured the building, Tia asked for clarifications about nearly every room and hallway. It seemed to me that this overconfidence in her own abilities might be an issue to further explore.

Counselor: This will just be a good way to get really familiar with your classrooms and be able to get to know another student right away.

Tia rolled her eyes and reluctantly agreed. Before I sent her on her way, I showed her how to open her locker, which she again adamantly denied needing any sort of help with. I showed her once and allowed her to try, but she could not get it open. I wrote down specific directions and her combination, which she successfully used to open her locker, then I sent her off with her student ambassador for the day. She returned two more times that day saying that she could not get into her locker despite my written directions and demonstration just hours ago, so I gave her other written directions to try for the day.

Over the next few weeks, this was just one of the many struggles Tia presented with.

Knowing we would need support from Mom to be able to work effectively with Tia, I made extra effort to keep her informed. We spoke on the phone often about my concerns regarding Tia's overconfidence in certain areas, her slipping grades, and bizarre interactions with others in our building. One example that comes to mind of the latter was when Tia came to my office about an afterschool issue she had the day before.

Tia: That girl kept telling me I had to leave, but I missed my bus so where else was I supposed to go?

Counselor: That girl? Who is "that girl"?

Tia: You know, that girl out there (pointing toward the front of the counseling office).

Counselor: You mean Mrs. Sherman? The one who does activities and attendance?

Tia: Yes.

Our conversation went on long enough for me to realize that in the four or five weeks that Tia had been with us at school, she could not remember the names of most of her teachers or the other staff with whom she came into contact on a daily basis. It was this type of information that I would pass to her mom whenever it came up, so that Mom could get a good picture of the unique needs that Tia was demonstrating to us. Her mom decided to get Tia and herself involved in therapy outside of school; however, she was still defensive when it came to personal matters, so she was not at all interested in signing a release of information to allow the therapist and I to speak. I was disappointed by that; however, I respected her wishes. I vividly remember the first day that Tia attended therapy before school. I was in an assembly in our gym when a call came over my walkie saying that I was needed. Tia's mom had brought her to school and had been arguing with her in the parking lot for twenty minutes, trying to get her to come into the building. I went outside to see if I could offer help, hoping I could convince Tia to come inside.

Tia: I'm not going in there.

Counselor: What's going on? Did something happen?

Tia: No, I went to therapy this morning, and I'm just not feelin' it.

Tia's mom: *Please!* Tia, just go into the building! I have to go to work!

Tia: Well, go to work!

Tia's mom: I can't. You need to get out of the car and go to school, and I need to go to work.

Tia: Well, you can call the cops if you want, cuz I'm not getting out.

I did my best to negotiate. I offered my office as a transition point. I offered check-ins during each of her classes for the day. I tried reasoning.

Counselor: Tia, it's clear your mom really needs to leave for work. Let's let her go and we can go inside and talk about how therapy went.

Tia: Nah, I'm not going in today.

Counselor: Tia, help me understand. What's going to be different tomorrow? My worry is that you'll feel the same tomorrow, and we need you in school to learn.

But Tia did not budge. I was floored. I'd always had success negotiating with school-resistant students, and oftentimes the parents enabled the behaviors by not even getting them to the parking lot. Tia's mom had done everything right. She was here. She took Tia to therapy in the morning and drove her to school straight after. Now Tia was digging her in heels, and neither her mom or I could not understand why.

Ultimately, Tia's mom took her home that day, clearly frustrated and unsure about what to do next.

The parking lot incident seemed to be a turning point in my relationship with Tia's mom. I told her I thought she had done everything right that day, and I really did my best to help. Tia's mom said she was grateful for my help and trusted that she could count on me when it came to these puzzling power struggles. She also decided to sign a release of information so I could connect with Tia's therapist to better support her in school. I would get to know that therapist well through many conversations about Tia; unfortunately, Tia grew to be a more complex puzzle than I ever expected. Her therapist agreed that a family approach was important, especially due to Tia's complicated history with her mom. Tia had lived with her dad her entire life and absolutely favored her father over her mother, who had been in and out of her life for most of her thirteen years. Tia viewed her mom as a cheater who abandoned her father, and she knew surprisingly descriptive details about their marriage prior to divorcing. This all led Tia to viewing her mother as someone who was untrustworthy and, at best, a formality in her life. Her therapist also told me that she was concerned about Tia's lack of truth telling and tendency to manipulate others, neither of which I had concerns about until Tia once mentioned to me that she "enjoyed manipulating" adults. Her therapist assured me that they would work on that as a family in their next sessions; however, Tia and her mom eventually stopped attending. We then reached the point at school in which we had provided the maximum amount of support we could give her in the general education setting. Since Tia's mom would not release any of her diagnostic paperwork from Conrad, a 504 plan would be difficult to put in place and likely insufficient in meeting Tia's needs. This is where working within school systems gets tricky. As a counselor, I did not want to refer yet another student of color for a special education evaluation, but I also knew that we had maxed out the supports that we could offer her. Tia wasn't doing well. Above all, I was concerned that Tia was expressing more and more frustration at school as time went on, hiding in the bathrooms to avoid going to class in the morning, saying that she was not interested in forming friendships with the other students, refusing to come to school at all, and showing more and more resistance toward her teachers when it came to schoolwork. Ultimately, we recommended her for a special education evaluation, and though her mother agreed with this recommendation in May, she never returned the proposal and unenrolled Tia from our school for the upcoming fall. Much to our surprise, in September, Tia walked through our front doors again, ready to start her ninth-grade year.

CASE DISCUSSION

The story of Tia and her family is a complicated one, at best. For many reasons, it became clear from the beginning that a family systems approach would be important in working with Tia. The first reason for this was that I realized in order to uphold the ethical standards of the American School Counselor Association (ASCA), I simultaneously had an obligation to respect Tia's autonomous rights, wishes, and confidentiality while also respecting the educational and parental rights of Tia's mom, especially since Tia was a minor (ASCA, 2016). This meant it was absolutely necessary to apply a theoretical approach that would assist me in working directly with Tia and indirectly with her mom, keeping open lines of communication and building trust with both Tia and her mom. This is what makes the work of school counselors so complicated; with this approach, it flips the notion that I work with roughly three hundred and thirty *students* into the sobering fact that I work with roughly three hundred and thirty *families*: parents, siblings, grandparents, aunts, uncles, cousins, and more. Additionally, I have come to discover that the ASCA School Counselor Competencies lists the word *parents* eleven times in describing how school counselors must collaborate with, understand the rights of, explain the benefits of school counseling programs, and consult with parents in order to develop, maintain, and provide a comprehensive school counseling program (ASCA, 2007). This again highlights the perspective that ASCA takes on working with students within the context of their families as not only beneficial but essential.

Another reason that I chose a family systems approach with Tia was because Tia did not exist in isolation. She existed *within* and *as a product of* her family system, which would have more impact on her individually than I ever could hope to have (Corey, 2013). This is why I began to partner with Tia's mom to discuss potential changes in Tia's context rather than just with Tia.

For example, the day after Tia refused to get out of the car, Tia's mom came to discuss the situation with me. It was clear that she felt exasperated and she was asking for ideas to help. I reflected and validated her feelings, and we talked about resources in the community that can support parents. I referred her to a parent support group held by a community partner; we also discussed the potential benefits of family therapy outside of school, which she moved forward with. Later I would partner with the therapist to help explore the option of having professionals come into their home to discuss dynamics and help Tia's mom build confidence in her own parenting approaches and skills. All of these things focused less on changing Tia and more on changing Tia's context, an approach encouraged by family systems theory (Corey, 2013).

Finally, adopting this theoretical approach became beneficial when it came to the hostility between Tia's parents. Tia's parents had been married at the time Tia was born but divorced shortly afterward, and Tia had lived with her father in another state for most of her life. Tia often brought up the hostility between her parents through comments and accusations that clearly paired her with her father and pitted her against her mother. This classic display of triangulation (two people in a triad joining forces against and cutting off the third person) was clearly forming a barrier to the positive, healthy development of Tia and her mom's relationship (Walsh, 2012). What I found most difficult in helping to challenge and break down this barrier were the logistics involved. I did have permission to connect with Tia's dad; however, his involvement in our work had been minimal, since he was in another state raising his other children and working full time. However, Tia's mom had made it clear that she was not happy about me connecting with Tia's dad when I originally had reached out to him to get background information at the time of Tia's enrollment. I found that simultaneously respecting the relationship I'd built with Tia's mom and adhering to the family systems approach of engaging the prominent members in Tia's family (including her dad) to be incredibly challenging. Ultimately, I placed precedence on respecting the relationship I had with Tia's mom and her wish to handle the relationship with Tia's dad on her own over directly involving Dad in these conversations. Instead, I worked to combat the triangulation effects through conversations with Tia, her mom, and their therapist, but this lack of communication and connection with Tia's dad would become one of my regrets when working with this family.

As I reflect on my time spent with Tia, I feel confident with my choice to spend such a vast amount of time developing my relationship with her and her mom. The family systems theoretical approach helped me to view Tia not as an individual without context to "fix," but as a valuable member in her family system, which had been shaping who she was from the moment she was born. To discuss and encourage positive changes in her context rather than within only Tia herself was one of the most important things that I felt I could do to support her as a counselor. However, I still look back on her story and question what I could have done differently to help. I feel confident in my work with Tia, her mom, and their therapist in discussing ways to foster a positive mother-daughter relationship, to build her mother's parenting skills, and to encourage Tia to advocate for herself at home. However, I absolutely wish I could go back and further involve Tia's dad in our work. I suspect that could have sparked further growth, especially since Tia trusted and felt much more secure in her relationship with her dad than she did with her mom. I also wonder if a recommendation for a special education evaluation was the right move. The data collected on her academics, behavior, and attendance suggest that it was, but since Mom ultimately decided against it, I wonder if there was a different approach to supporting her academics. Finally, I consider my relationship with Tia. She came to my office to ask questions often. Usually, it was to clarify our afterschool supervision policy or to see if she could switch classes because she didn't like the teacher. I'm curious, though, what it was that I was not doing for Tia. I wonder if she'd have an answer for me if I asked her now, or, if in Tia's mind, I wasn't the key to helping her unlock the answers to school, family, and happiness.

I don't know what is next for Tia. I hope for the best and trust in the theories and practices that we worked through together, because at a certain point, that is all I can do. What I know for sure is that she is a strong, independent force to be reckoned with, and I'm optimistic that if she continues to build her relationship with her mom, to work toward her goals day by day, and to seek out those with whom she connects, she will find happiness and success.

DISCUSSION QUESTIONS

1. In what ways could Tia's counselor have further involved Tia's dad? What strategies could be used to continue to build a positive relationship with Tia's mom in the process?
2. What are the responsibilities of school counselors, as defined by the American School Counseling Association, when it comes to students who struggle with coursework?
3. In what ways would you partner with Tia's therapist to support her at school?

4. Do Tia's unknown diagnoses play a role in how you would approach family systems work with her and her parents?
5. What responsibilities does Tia's counselor have to transition her into her ninth-grade year with a new counselor?

REFERENCES

American School Counselor Association. (2007). ASCA school counselor competencies. Alexandria, VA: Author.
American School Counselor Association. (2016). ASCA ethical standard for school counselors. Alexandria, VA: Author.
Corey, G. (2013). *Theory and practice of counseling and psychotherapy* (9th ed.). Pacific Grove, CA: Brooks/Cole Pub.
Walsh, F. (Ed.). (2012). *Normal family processes, fourth edition: Growing diversity and complexity.* New York, NY: The Guilford Press.

Chapter Twelve

Tara

The following case study took place at a high-achieving ninth through twelfth grade school in a medium-sized urban school district in the upper Midwest. The student body consisted of 65 percent white, 15 percent African American, 10 percent Latino, 8 percent Asian, and 2 percent Native American students, and the overall free and reduced lunch population was 35 percent. The school counselor–to–student ratio was approximately 1:450. I chose to focus on this case for two reasons. First, it represents the importance of attention to students' social and emotional needs, including family systems dynamics and home life, despite high caseload ratios that often create work conditions for school counselors that lead to "checking out" (at the very least) and burning out (in the long run). Second, the case demonstrates the increasing importance of school counselors, specifically white school counselors, to address racial and cultural needs of students in order to be effective in supporting high-achieving outcomes for all students.

As you read this case study, look for the following:

- What skills and knowledge did the school counselor utilize in order to build trust quickly with the student?
- How did the school counselor communicate high expectations for the student?
- How and with whom did the school counselor successfully collaborate in order to promote support and school success for this student?
- How did knowledge of family systems theory strengthen the school counselor's work with this student?

CASE STUDY INTRODUCTION

Tara was an African American student entering twelfth grade. Until eleventh grade, Tara always had lived on the city's north side with her mom. She traveled from this highly segregated, high-poverty neighborhood by city bus for more than an hour each way to her high school. Prior to her mom's death in eleventh grade, Tara did not have much of a relationship with her father, a high school dropout. Tara earned a 3.89 cumulative grade point average and scored a 27 on her ACT.

I was entering my fifth year as a school counselor at a high-performing secondary school on the opposite side of town from where I practiced for the first four years of my career. Previously I had been in a highly segregated kindergarten through eighth grade community school in an economically depressed neighborhood. At that school, the vast majority of my students were African American and qualified for free and reduced lunch. My students' needs were many and oftentimes basic: safety, stability, consistency, and adults who loved and expected the best from them. To say that my new placement was a culture shock would be an understatement. The neighborhood itself was lined with a continuous mature green canopy from boulevard trees. The housing stock was pristine with new construction on nearly every block. Near the school was an established and thriving small business center, which included yoga studios, a high-end grocer, movie theaters, and lots of fine dining restaurants. The shock wasn't simply adjusting to what existed outside the bricks and mortar of the high school. As I began to meet with my new colleagues and study school photos of students that were now on my caseload, I learned that most of the students with whom I would be interacting would be white. No longer would I be working in a segregated black cultural space; I would need to adjust to a much more multiracial reality, which included Spanish- and Somali-speaking families and students, middle- and upper-middle-class white students from the surrounding neighborhood, and African American students who opted into the school choice program and bused from across the city to attend. The latter circumstances provided Tara the opportunity to enroll at this high school.

I chose to focus on this case primarily because it highlights the potential impact that school counselors can have on students' experiences of school and their outcomes when attuned to the richness and complexity of their familial, social, and cultural existence. The cultural and racial diversity of U.S. students continues to increase. This increase is apparent whether we practice in rural or urban locations. The need for our profession to respond with cultural awareness and humility is apparent, as our students' outcomes depend on it. Utilizing family systems theory is helpful for school counselors who wish to connect in meaningful ways with students and the complex realities facing them. Creating strong, authentic relationships with students is a prerequisite for supporting their school success. Seeing students fully in the familial, social, and cultural contexts in which they exist is critical to building and maintaining trusting connections. The case study here illustrates that many otherwise caring adults missed an opportunity to connect with Tara following her mother's death and her subsequent grieving process. What she learned from those initial interactions was that school wasn't a place she could be seen fully or get the support she needed. School counselors are poised to listen to and understand our students, especially when it comes to their family systems, cultural backgrounds, and their current social contexts while at school.

INCIDENT

My initial meeting with Tara went well. I prepared for our session by double-checking my course credit evaluation, her transcript, and pulling the questions from our counseling department's senior meeting protocol. These questions were an attempt to draw out the breadth and depth of information needed from students for writing letters of recommendation. With a counselor-to-student ratio of 1:450—and being brand new to the school that year—I would surely need some tools and a system to effectively support students across the grade span with their various academic, college and career, and social and emotional needs. My preparation also included some thoughtful consideration about how to get to know Tara. Given the recent loss of her mom and the battle she had with other school staff about her decisions following that event, I wanted to demonstrate to her that I was someone who was open to relating to her as she was, someone whom she could trust.

Tara was refreshing. She was driven and assured. She came with her own checklist and a myriad of questions regarding scholarships and deadlines. Tara's diplomatic communication was apparent. She expressed feeling frustrated that people didn't understand her need to take time away and manage her grief on her own terms. She also shared that she didn't need the blessing or support from the adults at school; she knew what she needed. My initial impression was that she was independent and clear. I shared with her that I was glad to have this opportunity to meet her and was looking forward to the year we would have together. I thanked her for returning to a school even though she didn't feel supported by the adults. I expressed my hope that I could be helpful to her. As we wrapped up, I decided to explore with her what it was like for her to attend a mostly white school as an African American student. I knew it was a risk. We had just met, and I was a white counselor broaching the race conversation. The upper Midwest is not known for its open dialogue among white people about race relations. However, my question and curiosity were genuine. I wanted her to know that even though I am white, I am aware of and think about how race impacts our lived experience in the United States (Hutchinson, 2018). I wanted her to feel seen, and I believed it would help develop trust at the speed I needed it to grow (Covey, 2008). With only one year as her counselor and a few brief sessions ahead of us during that time, I couldn't afford to pass on the opportunity to learn more about her potential social and emotional needs (Covey, 2008). Tara responded positively. She paused thoughtfully and tipped her head to the side. She said, "no one at this school has ever asked me that before." She seemed truly struck and yet relieved. She shared that it was hard sometimes because she felt like it was such a white space that no one really acknowledged race or wanted to talk about it. She also talked about some of the pressure and loneliness she felt being one of the only students of color in her rigorous advanced placement coursework. Our conversation came to a natural end and she let me know she'd be in touch when she needed help with the next steps in the college admissions process.

A few days later, I received an email with information about a highly selective scholarship opportunity. This national scholarship required students to submit a comprehensive portfolio and include their top five schools (from the participating highly selective private college list). Tara fit the profile: high performing with a good GPA and ACT score, she was a student of color with economic need. I crafted an email to encourage her to apply and sent her the information. She wrote back and expressed interest.

School started. Following the initial rush of students requesting for schedule changes, I noticed an appointment on my calendar with Tara. Tara clearly knew how to access me and had the skill set to do so. I looked forward to checking in about how it felt to be back in classes again, get an update on her scholarship application, and explore whatever else she wanted to discuss. Tara was doing alright. She was feeling fine about her classes and was actually glad to be back at school. She saw our high school as an opportunity for her, a way out. It was a place where academic expectations were rigorous, and she could escape her depressed neighborhood. I asked her about how she managed the long bus ride to and from school. She shared that it really wasn't a hardship for her. She used that time to study or read. She liked that the city bus afforded her the flexibility to participate in afterschool clubs since she could jump on any route and get back home when it worked for her. Tara then opened up about what it was like during the last year after her mom got sick. She shared that she was the primary caregiver for her mom throughout her illness and decline. There were many days when her mom couldn't get off the couch. Tara described doing her homework on her laptop sitting next to her mom, who was too sick to interact much, in order to spend time with her and draw strength from her. She told me that her mom was the single biggest factor in who she was. Her commitment and resolve to do something big with her life—in journalism, policy, or social service—would result from her mom's faith and belief in her. It was incredible. I wondered how this young person could have such clarity and strength at this point, only a few months after her mom's death. Her resiliency was apparent. It struck me that this was the same person who wasn't heard when she tried to tell other adults at school what she needed a few months back. I reminded myself to let Tara lead, but I asked thoughtful questions when the moment felt right. We explored her current support network and how that had changed since her mom passed. Acknowledging the whole of her family system, I was also curious about her dad. She hadn't said much about him in our few meetings together, although she was living with him now. Knowing that Tara already faced several risk factors, I wondered how she was adapting and managing such a big change in her family system (Butler, Crespi, & McNamara, 2017). As I broached these topics, I kept in mind my original hope: to be someone who heard and supported Tara. When she responded to my inquiry about her father with a succinct response that suggested this wasn't an area of distress for her, I believed her. She told me that even though her dad did not graduate from high school, she saw that he worked hard all of his life and she wanted to get to know him now even if they hadn't had much of a relationship prior to her mom's death. I had to avoid the desire to probe further into an area that my cultural and class norms judged as stressful or concerning. For Tara, not knowing her father and then having the opportunity to get to know him now was simply a fact of life. And her priorities drove our work together. Before ending the session, we recapped her college and scholarship application to-do list, which included some upcoming deadlines in the coming weeks.

Two weeks passed and amid back-to-back appointments one morning, Tara popped into my office. I was surprised, as Tara usually set her appointments days ahead of time and rarely carried a sense of urgency in her affect. This day was different. She asked if I could see her right then. "Absolutely," I told her. I could sense the importance of this meeting for her and brought her into my office. As she sat down, I could see a heaviness about her. I wasn't sure what to expect or what she would say. She was holding a piece of paper in her hand and asked if it would be alright if she read a letter out loud to me. She was nervous and crying. With tears streaming down her face, she paused for what felt like several minutes. She eventually said, "this is so hard, I'm not sure that I can do it." She asked if I would read the letter instead of her reading it to me. I agreed. Her letter detailed a deep fear she had about sharing a long-held secret, but she knew it was time and that she had found someone she trusted enough to share it with. She was worried about being judged and shamed for what she was holding. Her secret was that her mom had been a severe hoarder while she was alive. Her letter was succinct and without many details. My mind was racing. My only reference point for hoarding was sensationalized visuals on TV. I checked my need to begin "fixing" the situation and my curiosity to ask question after question to round out the visual picture in my mind. I simply paused. This was big. She never before trusted anyone enough to share this, and she had risked so much by walking into my office and handing me this piece of paper. I eventually broke the silence with, "Thank you, Tara. Thank you for trusting me enough to share this with me."

Through tears and her own fear, she began sharing more details. She had lived with her mom in difficult conditions throughout her life, during her mother's illness and during the process of her mother's death. The house had become so cluttered that there were only tiny pathways between rooms. Near the end, she no longer could shower. Sometimes they lost power because bills went unpaid. She often slept on the couch with her mom because the hoarding had taken over the bedrooms. Mice traveled freely and abundantly around them. She was ashamed that it had gotten so bad and that she couldn't do anything about it when her mom was alive. Now that her mom was dead, she felt forced to confront the reality as an adult who had to manage the estate. To an extent, she was freed by not having her mom's perception and control playing out in her day to day, but now she was overwhelmed with the stress of having to deal with all the stuff in the house. She wanted to sell the house and go to college. She had no interest in living in or renting the property. Although this was a huge emotional challenge, it also required logistical guidance. I listened and empathized. I asked for her permission to consult with our social worker because I had no reference point or experience with resources that might be available for removing trash from houses. She agreed that help from other adults made sense. She felt some urgency to get back to class, and I let her know that I would do some digging and get back to her with some resources over the next few days.

A few days later, Tara and I met. She was doing okay. She was feeling lighter because she shared her secret and it was no longer her burden to carry alone. However, she was overwhelmed by the previously doable to-do list for college applications and scholarships. Dealing with her mom's house felt like the priority—and one that wouldn't be resolved quickly. The deadline for the competitive selective college scholarship she was planning to apply for was just two days away. She chided herself for not asking her teachers for letters of recommendation earlier. On top of that, she believed her teachers might not want to write the letters because she had taken last semester off and completed school online. She questioned whether these teachers really knew her well enough to write letters on her behalf. She was certain it was next to impossible to complete the application given all that had to be done. Listening to her hopelessness, I recognized her thinking was leading her down a path to underachievement. I knew this wouldn't stop her from going to college, because I knew she'd go somewhere, even if it was a modest start at the local community college. But I didn't want it to stop her from aspiring to and applying for those highly selective opportunities. "Undermatching" is a well-documented problem for students of color and students living in poverty in the United States (Jaschik, 2012). I wondered how I could support her and prevent her from becoming another high-achieving student of color who didn't apply for that selective college experience for which he/she totally qualified. I remembered what Tara had shared with me previously about how much she was inspired and strengthened by her mom's faith in her. I knew that with the shame surrounding the house, her mom's hoarding, and her own grief over her mom's death that her mom was already with us in the room. I wanted to draw on the positives and allow her grief to take shape in the form of honoring her mother as she faced this obstacle. I asked Tara what her mom would want her to do about the application if she was sitting there with us. Tara knew that her mom would want her to keep moving toward her goals, toward college. Her mom would want her to complete the application. She could certainly articulate that. But Tara was also expressing her own worries and shame about not having done it already. I wasn't certain how her teachers would respond this late in the game nor was I sure if I was pushing too hard given all that Tara had on her plate socially and emotionally. Yet Tara seemed to demonstrate a unique level of resilience at every turn, and I wanted to do whatever I could to instill hope and allow her to share her burden (the work of completing the application) with the caring adults in the building. "What is the worst thing that can happen to you if you ask teachers for letters of recommendation?" I asked. She paused. "Well, I guess they could say no." I continued, "And how would that feel to you?" She noted that it wouldn't be that big of a deal and that it's probably worth it to ask. I wasn't sure she was convinced of her plan about asking for recommendations or if she would complete the applications, but she seemed less stressed as she headed back to class.

Tara went on to complete the scholarship application and became a semi-finalist. Though she did not win a scholarship to one of her top five selective colleges, she was invited to several panel interviews and college campus visits at elite private colleges like Stanford and Sarah Lawrence as a semifinalist. In one of our final meetings, Tara remarked on how impactful and transformational these experiences were for her. During the final semester of her senior year, Tara received a full ride to a local private college. She also received a modest scholarship from the State School Counseling Association for the essay she wrote about the impact of our work together on her belief in herself and on her ability to complete such a daunting application during the height of her personal crisis. Following graduation, she served the mayor's office as a summer intern, focusing on communications and public relations.

CASE DISCUSSION

Working with Tara provided me an opportunity to work from a wholehearted place while addressing academic, postsecondary, and social and emotional domains. The American School Counselor Association (ASCA) Ethical Standards for School Counselors directs us to be "concerned with students' academic, career and social/emotional needs and encourage each student's maximum development" (ASCA, 2016). Tending to her family systems dynamics was simply one critical lens with which to approach the rich content that we worked through together. Although Tara acknowledged ways that I was able to support her and help her along her pathways, it's clear that Tara was her own reason for her success. My experience at this high school and with Tara reinforced for me the importance of school counselors engaging in our own professional development and personal reflection around cultural humility, social justice, and leadership work (Ratts & Greenleaf, 2017). As a white person, I engage in critical self-reflection regarding my own whiteness, the United States' history of white supremacy, and the current lived realities of my students and colleagues of color. Cross-cultural understanding is possible only when we, as professionals, have done our own personal work around identity and privilege. If we choose to overlook the importance of this work, we miss the opportunity to connect with our students on the level that they may need in order to truly thrive in our school community and to achieve at the highest levels they are capable. Ultimately, our effectiveness as leaders within our schools will be judged on our ability to advocate for our most vulnerable and at-risk student populations.

As I reflect on Tara, I am always struck by her resiliency as she transitioned to living with her father, who she did not know prior to her teenage years. I often have wondered what ways I would have approached working with her if her ability to adapt wasn't as strong as it was. Family systems theory focuses on understanding the family systems impact on how individuals behave. Tara's communication and behavior suggested her boundaries and differentiation of self were strong. For instance, the fact that her dad did not graduate high school was not going to negatively impact her belief in herself, her own relationship to school, nor her trajectory within her high school experience. Her strength and resilience allowed me to more easily focus on seeing her for whom she was in the world rather than focusing on her familial history that put her "at risk" for negative outcomes. The major goal of Murray Bowen's family systems theory is to reduce anxiety by addressing a variety of areas within family relationships. For Tara, her mother's death provided an opportunity to free herself from the past pattern of "fusing" with her mother and thereby protecting her mother's greatest secret—her hoarding (Brown, 1999).

In the context of supporting individual development through our counseling work with students, we are obligated to respect our students' family and cultural values, checking any sense of superiority or impulse to impose our own cultural, ethnic, or family values onto our students (ASCA, 2016). Understanding best practices in combating the ways that racism and classism negatively impact our students of color and students living in poverty is critical if we are to impact our most vulnerable students' outcomes. Understanding out students' barriers to success is only possible if/when we show up compassionately, curiously, and with an open mind to each session. With overwhelming caseloads and the ever-increasing demands of the job, it takes daily conscious effort to stay emotionally present for our students who may have no other trusted adult in whom to confide. Family systems issues are one of many compounding risk factors to be aware of as we connect with students and assist them in overcoming barriers to their academic and post-secondary/career success.

DISCUSSION QUESTIONS

1. How might family systems theory limit our work as school counselors as we focus on academic, postsecondary/career, and social/emotional development with students?
2. What if Tara didn't have the self-advocacy skills or the knowledge about how to access the school counselor?
3. What can school counselors do on an individual and a systemic level to support underrepresented students and to ensure that students are not "undermatching" with their postsecondary applications?

REFERENCES

American School Counselor Association. (2016). Code of Ethics for School Counselors. Alexandria, VA: Author.

Brown, J. (1999). 1999. Bowen family systems theory and practice: Illustration and critique. *Australian and New Zealand Journal of Family Therapy*, 20(2): 94–103.

Butler, S. K., Crespi, T. D., & McNamara, M. (2017). Family counseling in the schools. *Counseling Today*.

Covey, S. 2008. *Speed of Trust*. Free Press.

Hutchinson, C. (2018). How do white female therapists address racism? Blog post. Retrieved from www.psychedinsanfrancisco.com/white-female-therapists-address-racism/.

Jaschik, S. (2012, December 11). The missing students. *Inside Higher Education*.

Ratts, M. J., & Greenleaf, A. T. (2017, January 1). Multicultural and social justice counseling competencies: A leadership framework for professional school counselors. *Professional School Counseling, 21*: 1–9.

Part V

Solution-Focused Theory

Problem talk creates problems; solution talk creates solutions.
—Steve de Shazer

Solution-focused brief therapy (SFBT), a short-term therapeutic approach, is examined in the next three chapters. SFBT is commonly used by school counselors due to its direct and timely interventions. Because school counselors may be charged with caseloads of hundreds of students, SFBT is the often the most efficient and effective approach. With the counselor serving as a guide, SFBT helps students identify and clarify goals, identify solutions, and develop a plan for change.

As you read the next three chapters, note the specific questioning techniques, incorporation of empathy, and use of compliments, which help students to recognize their courage, strengths, and other virtues. These counselors focus on what the students can do, not what they cannot do, to help the students find solutions and make positive changes quickly. Explore how the school counselors assess the students' self-awareness and quickly establish rapport to build the collaborative counseling relationship. Finally, examine how the school counselor aids students in highlighting exceptions to their problems and continually provides positive feedback.

Chapter Thirteen

Britta

The following case study took place at a high-achieving kindergarten through eighth grade school in a small, urban school district in the suburbs of the metro area. The student body consisted of 90 percent white students. The school counselor to student ratio was approximately 1:600. I chose to focus on this case for several reasons. First, it represents the importance of attention to students' social and emotional needs, including family systems dynamics and home life. Second, this case highlights the importance of taking into account how students view their life and stressors. It's a reminder that students' feelings and perceptions are their reality. Additionally, the case demonstrates the increasing importance of solution-focused approaches in the school counseling role and the need to be strategic and work from a theory and framework. Finally, I believe it shows the need to be real and to challenge our students to try new things and be their own strongest advocate.

As you read this case study, look for the following:

- Solution-focused questions
- The student's ability to self-reflect
- Question prompts that challenge the student

CASE STUDY INTRODUCTION

Britta was a fun, smart, peppy, ten-year-old young lady who attended a small kindergarten- through eighth-grade charter school in rural Minnesota. The school itself had six hundred students. Classes were small, and students often stay in these small classes before moving on to high school. Britta had been on my radar since kindergarten. She was funny and outgoing but had a short fuse and often became angry. Things that would trigger her often were small.

She was an only child, born to parents who started a family later in life and who often took her along to many outings in which she primarily hung out with adults.

Most kids would not think twice about the problems Britta experienced; however, to her, these problems were relatively large. Britta was intuitive enough to know that her short temper and anger were not serving her well. In September of her fifth-grade year, she signed herself up to see me without prompting. She walked into my office one day and declared, "Mrs. Riz, I need help with my anger." I responded positively and asked her what she thought would be helpful. She decided on weekly meetings with me and wanted to make sure that she would tackle this issue head on. I told her that I admired her willingness to create change and asked her to set a goal for herself. Britta's goal was simple: "I cannot blow up and get annoyed with my family or my friends anymore." I honored her goal and scheduled weekly meetings for eight weeks, with the goal of figuring out how to help her to cope and deal with her anger.

INCIDENT

Britta and I established a mutual understanding that coping with her anger was something she needed to learn. It was also agreed that determining the extent of the problem was absolutely necessary in order for her to avoid exhausting her energy on things that she either couldn't change or were relatively small in the grand scheme of things. I let Britta know that anger might not be something she could "get rid of" but rather something she would have to cope with and find solutions for. Solutions meant having tools and resources to pull out when posed with triggering situations.

I learned that Britta often got mad at her dogs for being too noisy; it was so upsetting that she would come to school the next day still agitated and angry. When it came to peers, she could hold a grudge like no other. She once got so angry at a friend for talking too much about Pokémon that she cried in my office for more than ten minutes while screaming "I hate Pikachu" with clenched fists and giant tears. These problems were all real for Britta. I needed to figure out how to help her bring some cognitive and rational thoughts into her world so she could free herself from the suffering. Solution-focused strategies would help her the most. I was challenging Britta to think outside her world and to create an idea that she could take specific and measurable strategies to view her problems differently.

Britta and I started by whiteboarding her feelings. She learned quickly that she was oftentimes angry about a number of things, and the last thing to strike a nerve was what set off her anger. Britta's feelings would often take over long before conscious thought. When she was calm and centered, she could tell you how silly it was to cry or get angry about dogs being annoying, since she knew they couldn't help it. When she was angry, however, she would see red, and it would be all their fault. I asked Britta, "Who is driving the bus of your life?" She looked at me like I was crazy. I let her know that we are all in charge of the way we feel, and no one can make us feel a certain way without our permission. I let Britta know that she was in charge of her feelings and her responses and that she could choose a different road that could help her to be less angry. I asked her if she wanted to continue to let her dogs or friends "drive her bus" and get her angry and upset. She said, "No way!" I warned her that it would be hard work but that we would create a recipe for "anti-anger." She was hooked. I guided her and helped her learn that responsibility lies within, and she had the power to not let her anger get ugly. First we needed to create a line or phrase that signaled her brain to slow down and think. Britta came up with, "Stop. Does this even matter?" Next, we needed an action that would slow her heart rate. We agreed that five deep breaths would start the calming state naturally. Finally, Britta agreed to say out loud, "If I choose to get angry, I lose my control; if I chose to move on I can be happy," working from the framework of solution-focused therapy (SFT). I wanted to be goal oriented, concise, and make sure things were clear for Britta and focused on what Britta was trying to work on (Corey, 2009).

In addition to SFT, I created some concrete and developmentally appropriate visuals and resources for Britta. I utilized *The Zones of Regulation* workbook (Kuypers, 2011) to identify the zone she was in and to name her feelings. Another component of the literature/curriculum is to discuss the "size" of the problem: anything small could be resolved using our strategies; anything big (like someone hurting Britta or saying something mean) required an adult's help or extra attention. Britta quickly saw that many of her problems were small that she could solve on her own.

The hard part was putting our strategies into practice and tweaking them as needed. The next six weeks were rocky; Britta had some ups and downs, setbacks, and gains. Every week, good or bad, I asked her to rate herself on a scale from one to five regarding how well she was doing. Overall Britta always rated herself highly. Britta believed in herself and knew our strategies would work. October rolled around, and I took the opportunity to invite Britta's parents to a conference with Britta. Her parents were aware of the meetings Britta and I had been having and were happy to talk about her progress in person. After sharing with them the objective plan, we also talked about the importance of Britta hanging out with kids her own age outside of school. Britta's parents were baffled when I brought this up; they encouraged her to have friends over. Britta acknowledged that she knew her parents were supportive of her having friends over, but she was afraid that she would get angry and her friends would never want to come over again. Everyone realized in that moment that communication was necessary and that we could create a solution together. Britta's mom and dad put their arms around Britta and agreed to help. I shed some more light on the big-picture goals and ideas that Britta hoped to accomplish. Providing framework and introducing theories to families is strategic and useful: when parents are aware of the counselor's strategies, they quickly can incorporate them into the home. The family teamed up on the plan to actively use Britta's strategies at home with her in order to foster her confidence. This led to her parents setting additional goals for Britta, primarily having friends over. This shows that when you continue to build on solutions and strengths, motivation naturally occurs, and the student has the desire to continue working toward his or her goals.

After eight weeks, Britta was breathing, using strategies, and taking overall control of her anger. She no longer was crying and ruining her days. I believe a mixture of scaling and SFT, along with compassion and positivity, helped Britta. Importantly, Britta also had the will and desire. Britta and I continued to check in and connect every other week to maintain contact. By February I was seeing less of her, other than hugs and high fives in the hallway. The biggest reward was when Britta told me in the spring that she taught a friend her strategies and thought of herself as an "anger expert"; she had even had a sleepover during spring break and it was "awesome"! The American School Counselor Association (ASCA) national model asks counselors to be mindful of their services and what falls under the school counseling scope of practice. I believe that an eight-week intervention with a solid SFT framework is a reliable and measurable theory to track goals and outcomes.

The biggest learning opportunity that I took away was that everyone's problems matter. Even relatively small problems mean something to children, and counselors should strive to acknowledge that they aren't silly but rather have them determine for themselves their best strategies for dealing with them. Counselors get to be the passenger riding along to help, but the student can steer. Kids are smart: they know often their own struggles. We don't always have to point them out; they often will find their way to seek help when they are ready, especially if you make space for them and are visible in your schools in a way that is positive.

DISCUSSION

My theoretical approach was based on the key characteristics of solution-focused therapy: its brevity and focus on goals. The student in this case took control over her own goals and she was in the position to take responsibility and track her own growth. The counselor's job was to ask strategic, guiding questions to enable the student to determine if she was challenging her previous thoughts and processing the psychoeducation that was taught during the sessions. I believe that students are often "given" goals by well-meaning adults in their lives; the ASCA asks us to challenge that notion and think about individual student planning. When we think about what an individual needs and wants, we should be ask the source. Let's say that the student sets a goal that is not deemed a valid goal for based on what outcomes they hope to achieve (spoiler alert: adults do this all the time, too). Solution-focused therapy can help students to look at their stated goals more critically, teasing and working out strategies that are successful by examining their experiences and drawing upon what is effective. As school counselors, we always should ask ourselves, "What are this student's strengths?" Great goals are not derived from looking at weaknesses, although they certainly can be taken into consideration. Both SFT and ASCA challenge us to look at what makes students exceptional, and that often lies in their gifts (Dollarhide & Sagnik, 2012).

DISCUSSION QUESTIONS

1. How can you align ASCA and SFT into your comprehensive school counseling program?
2. What other considerations could have been made if Britta didn't meet her goal? How could you take the SFT model a step further with Britta and her family?
3. What happens when you don't have a student who is self-aware? What would you do if you had a student who was unaware of how his/her problems affected his/her life?

REFERENCES

Corey, G. (2009). *Theory and practice of counseling and psychotherapy.* Australia: Thomson/ Brooks/Cole.

Dollarhide, C. T., & Sagnik, K. A. (2012). *Comprehensive school counseling program: K–12 Delivery systems in action.* Boston: Pearson

Kuypers, L. (2011). *The zones of regulation: A curriculum designed to foster self-regulation and emotional control.* San Jose, CA: Social Thinking Publishing.

Chapter Fourteen

Mohamed

This chapter is based upon a compilation of middle school clients to provide an example of how a counselor utilized solution-focused theory (SFT). The primary SFT tenets included in this case involve being curious about clients, avoiding assumptions, working with clients to meet their needs, and empowering them to act.

As you read this case study, look for the following:

- Client- (student-) directed dialogue
- Counselor asks questions to guide the client (student) in identifying the concern/issue
- Counselor building on client (student) rapport
- Counselor drawing attention to times the student already has solved this issue
- Counselor helping the client (student) recognize exceptions or times when the concern/issue wasn't present

CASE STUDY INTRODUCTION

The case study is set in a diverse suburban middle school. There are two thousand sixth-, seventh-, and eighth-grade students. Approximately 50 percent of the students in the school identify as white, 25 percent identify themselves as black, 10 percent identify as Hispanic, and the remaining 15 percent identify as Asian, Native American, or mixed race. There are four school counselors who work with the students at the school to provide assistance in academics, social support, personal issues, and career development.

INCIDENT

I was in the cafeteria monitoring lunch when I noticed shouting and laughing from one of the tables filled with seventh-grade boys. Lunch duty in one of the largest middle schools in the state is always exciting; however, the interaction at this table appeared to require adult attention. As I approached the table it was clear that Mohamed, a twelve-year-old seventh-grade student, was upset. In reaction to the conversation that his classmates were having, Mohamed sat with his arms crossed and his head down. I stood near the table for a few seconds to listen to the exchanges. "Can you believe he has Velcro on his shoes?" said one of the boys as the rest of the group laughed hysterically. Another boy chimed in, "He probably got them from his grandpa's closet." More laughter ensued, and I realized the boys were talking about Mohamed's shoes.

I immediately intervened and told the boys that they needed to settle down as lunch was coming to an end soon. I addressed the boys by saying, "Hey guys, the comments I'm hearing don't sound like jokes, even if you think it's funny. We don't treat each other that way at our school. It's the end of lunch and you need to get going to class, but I'm going to be chatting with you guys later." I asked Mohamed if he was OK, and he gave me a shy smile and a nod. Even though I wasn't convinced he was OK, I reminded all the boys to be respectful toward each other as I walked away from the table. I planned to follow up later individually with Mohamed to avoid putting him in an uncomfortable situation in front of his peers. I know that students do not want to "snitch" or appear uncool in front of their peers and likely will not report being mistreated in that setting.

As the seventh-grade school counselor and primary support for Mohamed, I knew I needed follow up to get more details about the situation. How much had it impacted Mohamed? Had he tried other things to make it stop or address his peers? Is the teasing reciprocated or just one way?

He came to my office and I greeted him at the door by asking how he was doing and was met with a typical seventh grade response: "I'm good." I knew from my previous work with Mohamed that his friends enjoyed teasing each other, but this banter had occasionally made Mohamed feel attacked rather than valued as a friend. I knew that Mohamed's family was not wealthy but he had clean clothes to wear and food to eat. In the past I had mediated conversations with Mohamed and some of his friends when some of their teasing criticized another student's family life. I knew that Mohamed did not enjoy being teased about his family's economic situation. I had a feeling that the current situation in the lunchroom had something to do with this, but I didn't want to project my ideas or thoughts onto Mohamed.

"I know you say you're good, but when I saw you in the cafeteria earlier, I saw your head down and it did not look like you were happy with what was going on with your friends," I started the conversation as Mohamed and I sat down across from each other. Remaining curious about my client rather than projecting my assumptions is a key component of SFT (Gillen, 2005). Using observations and questions, rather than assumptions, allows clients to present their thoughts or feelings. Mohamed responded to my question, "It's just my friends. They were teasing me about my new shoes. I know they were joking, but I was kind of mad at them." My goal now is not to give the client an answer to his presenting problem; instead I want to help Mohamed think through ways to reach a solution that works for him (Lipchik, 2002). For instance, by asking Mohamed questions such as, "Do you want things to be different?" "What are you willing to do?" and "What would be helpful for you?" I empowered him to think about outcomes and solutions. To stimulate this thought, I asked Mohamed, "So what happened today when you were feeling that way?" His response: "Well, I didn't really say anything because I didn't want to get into an argument with them. They were already making me feel dumb. I just hate it when they make fun of people who are different than them. Why does it matter what shoes I'm wearing?"

Mohamed's response to my question opened a variety of avenues for conversation. However, the focus is on the issue most pertinent to the client, so it's essential to bring the conversation back to the client, allowing him to guide the dialogue (Bonnington, 1993). I inquired about previous situations Mohamed had experienced as an opportunity for growth. "Have you felt this way before when hanging out with your friends?" I asked. "It sounds like this isn't the first time it has happened." This allowed Mohamed to review previous situations when his friends were teasing each other and may have taken things too far with their joking. It also provided Mohamed an opportunity to consider how he handled that situation and whether he was satisfied with the outcome of it.

"Yeah, they were making fun of Kobe's shoes last week, so I told them to stop," Mohamed said without much thought. "We roast each other a lot, but sometimes they take things too far." I responded, "So, when you told them to stop, what did they do?" This line of questioning caused Mohamed to think deeper about the situation and begin to come up with possible solutions. Allowing clients to lead the conversation toward their goal is vital to ensuring that we are not assuming what they want to do or needlessly offering advice. Instead, we focus on the skills and abilities that the clients have utilized successfully in other similar situations and let them build on past successes.

Mohamed responded after a short pause, "They stopped talking about Kobe's shoes, but it feels like they are always making fun of somebody." At this point, I decided that I needed to focus on the presenting problem: Mohamed's friends making fun of his shoes. "So, it sounds like your friends are pretty receptive when you ask them to stop teasing other people. Would you agree that they usually listen if you ask them to stop?" Rather than skipping ahead to suggest he try that behavior once again, I collaborated with Mohamed to further explore his goal. I asked him to process the possible solutions to see how to work through this together.

CASE DISCUSSION

The most immediate and simplest choice could be to step in and offer support to or mediation for Mohamed. Although this seems like an obvious solution, it wouldn't be the best solution for Mohamed and deviates from another key tenant of SFT. It is vital that we allow our clients to explore options that work for them (Lipchik, 2002). Encouraging Mohamed to think about previous situations lets him determine the skills he possesses to solve the situation. He may choose to ask his friends to stop teasing, thereby reinforcing his own problem-solving skills. If Mohamed wanted to do something different but was struggling for ideas, we could have explored other possible solutions that have worked for Mohamed in similar situations. Recognizing past experiences and applying them to new situations is an SFT assumption that enables small changes to lead to bigger change (Gillen, 2005; Lipchik, 2002).

A key here is to help a client move toward a solution without defining it for them. This is often referred to as not "working harder" than your client. I could have easily suggested to Mohamed that I mediate the conflict and settle the issue. The problem with this approach is that ultimately Mohamed and his friends are not required to engage in the process beyond the initial mediation. If I work with them as they self-mediate and explore their boundaries, they are empowered to solve their own issues. I want to work as hard as my clients but not harder.

As my conversation with Mohamed continued, I asked, "What would be helpful for you right now?" The purpose of this question was to refocus Mohamed on the takeaway items from the session as a way of empowering him. Mohamed responded, "I don't know if I really need anything. I just want my friends to leave me alone and stop teasing everyone." This presented me with an opportunity to wrap up the conversation, so I asked him, "Well, would you be able to ask them to stop if they continue bothering you? It sounds like that has been working for you so far. If you feel like things are getting any worse, I know you understand that you can either find an adult in the cafeteria or let me know. But it sounds like you have plenty of skills to solve this yourself. So, those things that are working for you now, would you be willing to keep doing those?" This provided Mohamed with a solution to the presenting issue by recognizing times he had successfully resolved conflict, reinforced skills he already possessed, and still gave him the opportunity to come back if he needed anything else from me. My final statement, (to keep doing those things that are working) was purposely obtuse. Mohamed needed to recognize the issues he thought worked for him and remind himself about actions he had taken. In this final statement I removed myself from the solution and gave the credit to Mohamed for doing things that helped him solve his problem (Lipchik, 2002).

An important aspect of a school counselor's work is to follow up with students. This doesn't always require a formal office meeting. For instance, a quick check-in with Mohamed during lunch at a later date could work. Using questions such as "How did everything turn out?" or "How did you get that to happen?" offers him the opportunity to reassess the situation and create a new solution if necessary. When other issues arise for Mohamed and his lunch friends, this experience can be valuable to draw upon to help Mohamed reach a new solution that works best for him.

DISCUSSION QUESTIONS

1. How does the counselor's relationship with the client impact their ability to effectively apply SFT theories?
2. Why is it important for the counselor to provide feedback, but not advice or solutions for the client?
3. What ways did the counselor help Mohamed think about the issue and reach a solution?
4. Why is it valuable for counselors who utilize SFT to follow up with their clients?

REFERENCES

Bonnington, S. B. (1993). Solution focused brief therapy: Helpful interventions for school counselors. *School Counselor, 41*(2), 126–28.

Gillen, M. C. (2005, May 3). Providing efficacy for solution-focused theory in school counseling programs. *Journal of School Counseling, 3*(2), 1–14. doi: http://www.jsc.montana.edu/articles.

Lipchik, E. (2002). *Beyond technique in solution-focused therapy: Working with emotions and the therapeutic relationship*. New York, NY: Guilford Press.

Chapter Fifteen

Hannah

One of the things I love most about my job is the ability to watch my students change and grow over time. The overt changes of adolescence are apparent and obvious; the small changes that happen over time are easily overlooked. Yet teens are changing all the time! Whom they are one year is not whom they will become. Often even teens themselves do not recognize the changes that are occurring within them because everything feels weird, uncomfortable, and new. Additionally, just when they think they have figured "it" out—"it" being friendships, emotions, dating, school, their body—something changes and messes it all up again. Being a teenager is like riding an out-of-control emotional roller coaster that drops, spins, and turns when least expected.

To add to the confusion, adolescence is the bridge between being a child and becoming an adult. Though they want to be treated like adults, their brains are not prepared to function as adults. The prefrontal cortex, which is responsible for decision making, executive functioning, attention, and memory, is not fully developed until individuals are in their mid-twenties (Siegel, 2013). Even though it is normal for teenagers to explore their independence in order to find where they "fit," it can be difficult to balance letting teenagers make their own mistakes and guiding them in the right direction (Siegel, 2013). Teenagers want to make decisions independently (or with input from their friends), but they still need adults in their life to help them. I think of the relationship between teenagers and parents like dance partners: sometimes we have to give teenagers the space to lead; other times adults lead and teenagers have to follow. However, this "dance" between dependence and independence can often lead to a tug of war, with each partner fighting over who leads. If parents lead too often, teenagers may feel stifled and limited. In fact, it is common for teenagers to struggle with identifying and connecting to their locus of control. It often seems as if situations are being "done to them" and they have no control over what is happening. Sometimes that is true. However, teenagers have more control than they understand: they have the power and capacity to decide how they think, feel, and respond to every situation. It is empowering for them to realize that they can find solutions to their problems and make changes in their life.

For this reason, the solution-focused counseling theory can be a powerful approach for teenagers. One of the core tenets of solution-focused counseling is that clients are the experts—they identify the goals and the paths that they want to take to reach their goals (Egan, 2007). It is not often that adults defer to teenagers as experts. Yet that is why this approach is so meaningful. Teenagers have strengths, resources, and wisdom that they can use to solve their own problems. Instead of being told how to solve a problem by some-one else, teenagers can focus on solutions that fit their own unique experience of the world. Solution-focused counseling allows teenagers to tap into past successes and apply those solutions to current problems. Letting teens take the lead in this process not only fosters a cooperative relationship but allows teens to feel more in control of their life. I am often struck by the impact of solution-focused counseling on the growth of my students. It dramatically changes the dynamic of the counseling relationship. Rather than leading the process, I walk alongside my students, noticing and bringing attention to their strengths and solutions. It is amazing to watch them come to the realization that they already know what to do.

As you read this case study, look for the following:

- Consider effective approaches to working with a student living with selective mutism
- Recognize opportunities to advocate for the student with school staff
- Note the importance of building a strong student-counselor relationship
- Identify solution-focused techniques utilized by the school counselor

CASE STUDY INTRODUCTION

As a fresh-faced school counselor, I was ecstatic to start my first "real job" at a small, rural school. I had a multitude of ideas and was ready to put them into action. Being the only school counselor for grades seven through twelve, I was looking forward to building long-term relationships with my students. I was excited by the freedom I had to create my own comprehensive school counseling program. Then reality happened: there were already established roles that were expected of me, many of which were "non-counseling tasks" (according to the ASCA national model). My head was swimming and this was weeks before the students even showed up! I remember thinking to myself, "how am I supposed to do all this stuff *and* meet the needs of my students?" In that moment, I decided that I would prioritize my students' needs before anything else. After all, my students were the reason I became a school counselor.

The following case follows the five-year journey of a school counselor as she develops a positive relationship with a struggling student and utilizes a solution-focused approach to support her student in achieving her full potential.

INCIDENT

I can still remember the first time I heard about Hannah. I was organizing my new office when the special education director stopped by to check on me. After some casual conversation, we started talking about the student supports available within the school. He shared information about the special education program and 504 plans before shifting the discussion to students. He was giving me background information on a few "high fliers" with Individualized Education Plans (IEPs) when he exclaimed, "And what are you going to do about Hannah?!" With 450 students on my caseload, I needed him to be more specific. "Who is Hannah?" I asked. As I found out, Hannah was a rising eighth grader whose teachers were at a loss with what to do with her. Hannah struggled academically and rarely completed her homework; although she had a small group of friends, she did not feel like she had an adult at school that she could trust. In reality, many of the adults at school were so frustrated with her that they had given up on her: "She won't talk to me." "She won't participate in class." "She barely does her homework." And the list of things that Hannah "didn't" and "wouldn't" do went on. I learned that Hannah lived with selective mutism, although it was unclear if it was ever officially diagnosed. Selective mutism is a complex anxiety disorder in which individuals are unable to speak or communicate effectively in social settings, though they are able to speak in settings in which they feel safe, comfortable, and relaxed. In Hannah's case, school was a place she was unable to speak or communicate effectively, which made it difficult to assess her learning. In class, she completely shut down and "would not" speak. I also heard, "she can talk to her friends in the lunchroom, so she can't be that anxious." Everything I was being told made me curious about Hannah. Although selective mutism is rare, I worked with an elementary student living with selective mutism during my internship. I had felt completely helpless in my work with her because I was never able to connect with her. But Hannah intrigued me because she actually talked to her friends at school. It gave me hope—if she can feel comfortable enough to talk to her friends at school, then perhaps we can work on helping her feel more comfortable in her classes. My training in solution-focused theory had taught me to look for the exceptions—to find the times when the student has been successful.

Unfortunately, the times that she had been successful would create additional barriers for Hannah. She was evaluated for special education but did not qualify because her struggles were not evident in multiple settings. Although she clearly struggled in the classroom, she was observed talking to her friends in the lunchroom and her mom reported that she was talkative at home. Hannah had qualified for a Section 504 plan but was exited from the plan because "she didn't use the accommodations and it hadn't improved her performance anyway." The more I learned about Hannah, the more I looked forward to meeting her. It didn't take long.

By luck, Hannah's group of friends sought me out early and often. Sometimes Hannah came along when they talked with me. I always tried to engage her but I had very little success. I wasn't deterred—I felt that even if she sat silently in my office while her friends talked, at least she was in my office. I hoped that her access to me (through her friends) would be enough to lower her anxiety and help her feel safe with me. Her friends wanted to start a small counseling group and what a ragtag group we were. Hannah came to the group but sat silently, looking at the ground most of the time. She did not participate in any of the group activities; instead, she spent her time drawing or doodling. Yet she came to group every week and she continued joining her friends' individual sessions. I assumed she was coming to hang out with her friends or avoid class, but I also think she came to test me. I imagine she was there to answer her own questions and curiosity about me. Was I trustworthy? Was I judgmental? Was I helpful? Would I get upset with her if she continued to stay silent? I believed Hannah must be getting something from the time she spent with me, otherwise, why would she keep coming? I knew that she would not come if she did not feel valued or cared about. Teenagers are perceptive—they know when someone is not being genuine or authentic with them.

After about six months of silence, she started communicating with me—first by responding to my questions with head nods or shakes. Then she started writing her answers to my questions on Post-its. When she became comfortable enough to speak, she started responding with whispers of "yes," "no," or "I don't know." I felt limited to closed-ended questions with Hannah because every time I asked an open-ended question, she would sit in silence or respond with a shrug of her shoulders. It was clear she was scared to open up to me, but slowly we were building trust; I was starting to learn more about her. I knew she was a talented artist—I had seen her drawings and doodles during group. I asked her to share her art with me. She would bring her sketchbook and we would flip through the pages together. Usually, she was quiet while I commented on her talent or the characteristics of the drawing. Occasionally, she would quietly share how she was feeling while she was drawing or mention a detail that I had not noticed. Hannah was giving me glimpses of herself in brief, small moments. I learned that she loved video games. She was an only child and lived with her mom and stepdad. School did not motivate her at all. She was comfortable with her friends and only shared her true self with a handful of people she trusted. She was sad and lonely much of the time. Together, we were making slow progress on a relationship built on trust and patience.

While I continued to show up and meet Hannah where she was, she continued to frustrate teachers with her lack of participation and effort. Truthfully, her grades were atrocious. I can only imagine how difficult it would be to have a student like Hannah in class—in teachers' minds, she was "choosing" not to speak, participate, or complete her homework. There was clearly a lack of education and understanding about her symptoms, despite my efforts to help them accommodate her needs. Yet Hannah was making progress. She was starting to quietly improve in history and art. She even interacted with her art teacher a few times. One of the principles of solution-focused interviewing is that change is inevitable—it is not *whether* but *when* change will occur (Bannink, 2006). Outside observers could easily overlook her efforts but change was happening for Hannah. Additionally, only a small change is needed in a solution-focused approach (Bannink, 2006)—it was my responsibility to encourage Hannah to notice and find worth in these small changes.

Hannah had shown incredible growth since I first met her. She went from being a silent observer to a tentative participant. When Hannah was in tenth grade, she started to speak at school. Her friends told me they almost fell out of their chairs the first time they heard her respond to the teacher taking attendance. The teachers echoed the same reactions as Hannah's friends—they simply could not believe it. Here was a girl who had been silent most of her educational career and she was giving presentations in front of her entire class. She did it quietly, but she was doing it. One teacher said he could not believe she was the same person. It was like a door had been unlocked and cracked open—each year, the door opened a little bit more until it was wide open. I marveled at her growth and wondered what had made the difference for her. I assumed that maturity and confidence had contributed to the changes, but I felt that positive relationships with adults had significant impact. However, it was difficult to know what lead to the changes because Hannah still struggled to articulate her thoughts and feelings. I asked in many different ways what had changed, how she had done it, what she was doing differently. I continued to be met with a shrug of her shoulders and an "I don't know."

Although Hannah had improved her participation in class, she was still struggling to actually pass her classes. As a sophomore, she was already behind in her graduation requirements, as she had failed several of her ninth-grade classes. It was like a snowball rolling downhill—the pattern continued, and she fell further behind in tenth and eleventh grade. Insanity is doing the same thing over and over again and expecting different results (Einstein, as cited in Bannink, 2006). It seemed like we had the same conversation over and over. We would review her graduation requirements and discuss the classes she was behind in. We would come up with a credit recovery plan: putting classes back into her schedule and signing her up for night school or summer school. Sometimes she would follow through with night school and summer school, other times she would not. Even though we had a positive relationship, it still felt like she was resisting. Solution-focused counseling emphasizes that if something does not work, do something else (Corey, 2005). So I tried every approach that I could think of. We created an after-school homework plan and we set SMART—specific, measurable, attainable, relevant, and timely—goals. we created a course plan for her last two years of high school, we talked about the future lifestyle and career she wanted, we built in rewards for passing grades, we had meetings together with her teachers, we had meetings together with her mom. We continued to revisit and revise these approaches each year. Finally we hit the point of no return.

The sun was shining on a cool spring day. I had scheduled a meeting with Hannah and her mom to discuss Hannah's graduation requirements. I am an eternal optimist—I wholeheartedly believe in my students' abilities and potential; I refuse to be the person who tells them they cannot achieve their dreams. But on that day, it felt like I would have to do just that for the very first time; I was dreading the conversation I was about to have. It was still a year away, but after analyzing her transcript, it seemed there was no possible way Hannah would be able to graduate with her class the following year. Although this was not going to be a surprise to Hannah or her mom—I had been sharing my concerns about her not graduating on time since ninth grade—it still was difficult to cross the threshold from "may not" graduate to "will not" graduate. Despite all the progress Hannah had made, I felt like I had failed her.

I thanked Hannah's mom for coming and explained the purpose of the meeting. "We are here to discuss Hannah's graduation requirements and my concerns about her graduating on time next spring." Hannah and her mom listened while I showed them Hannah's transcript and reviewed her graduation requirements. For most of the meeting, both of them just listened. Occasionally, Hannah's mom would exchange silent glances with Hannah. Each time I would see Hannah sink lower into her seat and stare more intently at the ground. It was like I was watching Hannah regress right in front of me—she became the eighth-grade version of herself, a silent wallflower. After what seemed like forever, it was the moment of truth.

"This is difficult to say, but I just don't see how Hannah can graduate next year with her class. She's just too far behind." The words hung in the air. Finally, Hannah's mother looked at her and said, "Hannah, I don't understand how you have gotten to this place. I know you. I know that you are more than capable of passing your classes. There is no reason you should be at risk of not graduating. You have so much potential." Hannah sat silently looking at the ground.

"Hannah, I have to agree with your mom—you have so much potential. When I met you, you wouldn't even talk to me or participate in class. Now you are giving presentations in front of your class, you're talking to your teachers, and you're talking to me. We believe in you because you have shown us what you can do." Hannah continued to stare at the ground.

"So what are our options? What does she need to do to graduate on time?" her mom asked.

"We can take a look at the available options. I have to be honest, even if she does night school every semester, maxes out her summer school classes, and takes some classes online, I am still not sure Hannah will graduate on time." I was trying not to let my skepticism shine through but it was difficult.

"Hannah, I know you to be a talented, kind, and capable young woman. Your mom and I can come up with a plan to help you graduate on time, but we would be leaving out the most important person in this room—you. What is it that you want to work toward?" Hannah continued her silence. "You are the expert on yourself. You already have the solutions within you—we are here to help you realize what works for you and help you do more of that. Consider art. You are finding success in art and completing all of your work all of the time."

"That's because I like art," she said softly.

"Ah ha! She speaks! Yes, you like art and you are a very talented artist. It sounds like you care about it, therefore you are motivated to finish your work. Besides just liking the class, what are you doing differently in art?"

"I don't know. It's just easier for me to do. It doesn't feel like work to me. Plus, I really like Mrs. Donovan."

"OK. That's helpful to know. Let's talk about history. That is one class that you have been successful in almost every year of high school. How are you doing that?" Hannah was quiet. I could tell she was thinking and I was encouraged that she hadn't fallen back on her usual "I don't know" response. This was something new.

"I guess . . . umm . . . I guess with history maybe it's because I kind of like what we talk about in class. And Mr. Johan is pretty nice and I have had him for two years in a row so I feel like I know him better. He gives us time to get our work done. He lets us work with our friends as long as we are working on homework."

"Wow, Hannah. You took your time to think about that and shared some really important information about what helps you. Let me make sure I understand you. It sounds like the teacher is important—if you like the teacher, then it makes it easier for you to get your work done."

"Well, kind of. I like all my teachers but . . . umm . . . I don't want to sound mean but . . . well, it seems like some teachers care more about me than others. Like Mr. Johan and Mrs. Donovan. I have had them for more than one class and I feel like they really care about me. They encourage me and it helps. And I know how they run their classes so I kind of know what to expect from them." I was ecstatic. This was the most reflective I had ever seen Hannah, and I was getting a lot of essential information from her. In addition, she had confirmed what I had been wondering: relationships mattered to her.

"Alright, I want to make sure I understand so correct me if I get anything wrong. When you feel cared about, when you like what you're learning, when you know what to expect from your teachers, and when you have the opportunity to choose who you work with, those are the times you are most successful."

"Yeah, and when I am able to finish my homework at school."

"Well, then, I think we're onto something here. I know we haven't discussed a credit recovery plan yet but we will get to that. I want to know more about how you view the graduation situation. What are your best hopes for this situation?"

"I want to graduate with my friends."

"That sounds like an important goal for you. What difference would that make for you if you were able to graduate with your friends? What difference would it make for your mom?" Hannah's mom spoke up. "I am already proud of you but if you were to graduate with your friends, I would be even more proud of your hard work and effort to be able to do that."

"If I could graduate with my friends, I wouldn't feel left behind. Some of my friends are thinking about going to college and I don't know if I want to. I feel left out and kind of lonely because I can't talk about that stuff with them. If I didn't graduate with them, I would feel abandoned, even though it would be my own fault." Hannah started to cry. Her mom reached over and held her hand.

"It sounds like you are worried about losing your friends and being alone. Perhaps graduating with your friends is a way that you can stay connected to them. Is that right?" Hannah nodded her head. "Well, the good news is that we already have some ideas about what is working in the right direction. Building relationships with teachers so you feel comfortable with them and you understand what to expect from them. Being able to make personal connections helps you to like what you are learning. And being able to have some choice about when, where, and with whom you work on homework is helpful to you. This is a good start. On a scale of ten to zero in which ten is meeting your goal of graduating on time with your friends and zero is the worst moment you've experienced, where are you now?" Hannah thought for a while.

"I guess a one or two because I am so far behind and I don't know if it's even possible for me to graduate on time."

"I can understand how you might be feeling that way. Let me ask you it a different way: on a scale of ten to zero in which ten means 'I am willing to give it my all' and zero means 'I have no motivation at all,' how motivated are you to solve this problem and reach your goal?"

"Hmm . . . well, when you put it that way, I think I am a seven or eight. I want to say ten because I care about this, but I don't want to get my hopes up." Once again, I was elated by how much Hannah was sharing. I felt we had reached a real turning point for Hannah.

"That's fair. This seems pretty important to you because you're willing to work hard to solve this problem. Going back to your goal for a minute, what would be one sign that you are on the right track to reaching your goal?"

"I would be getting my homework done and turned in." I pushed her for more ideas, "What would I see you doing differently then?" "I would be finishing my work in all my classes instead of just art and history."

"How are you going to do that? What are some things you're already doing?"

"Well, if I don't finish my history homework in class, then I usually do it when I get home. And sometimes I'll call my friends and talk to them while I'm doing my work." I couldn't believe how much we were covering in such a short amount of time. I had asked these same questions so many times before and was not able to get anything remotely close to this from Hannah. "That's a great start, Hannah. I'm wondering two things: (1) what and who can help you keep this goal in view? and (2) what and who may be barriers to your success?"

"My mom and you can help me. My friends can help me, too, but they also could distract me sometimes. And video games." Hannah's mom agreed with this statement, "Oh yes. She *loves* her video games." We laughed together and Hannah seemed to brighten.

Together, we talked with Hannah about what steps she thought she could take to reach her goal. Then we created a rigorous credit recovery plan for Hannah. I was still skeptical that it was even possible for her to reach her goal but I kept my thoughts to myself. I had noticed a change in Hannah. She seemed to finally understand that it was up to her to bring about the change so she could meet her goal. Additionally, she seemed sufficiently motivated to work for it. And, boy, did she work! Hannah started her credit recovery plan that spring and summer—and she followed through with it. We started meeting weekly during her senior year. Every week, I asked her to scale her progress toward her goal, as well as her motivation. We reflected together on what was working and what needed to be changed. Hannah and I met with teachers quarterly to discuss her progress and to give Hannah a chance to share what helped her find success in their classes. Hannah continued to work diligently on her credit recovery plan all year. Through her hard work and effort, she walked across the stage in June with her friends. I thought it would take a miracle—as it turned out, it just took Hannah.

CASE DISCUSSION

According to James Comer, "no significant learning can occur without a significant relationship" (Payne, 2008). It was clear from when I first met Hannah that a trusting relationship would be essential to any work I hoped to do with her. As a new counselor, it was difficult to know exactly how to build a relationship with someone who would not talk to me. I often questioned myself: Am I asking too many questions? Does she feel like I am expecting her to answer? Should I expect her to answer? Should I skip over her in group so I don't make her feel uncomfortable? Am I ignoring her because she never talks? Is it better to talk to her directly or talk about her with her friends? Should I pretend like she is answering my questions? Should I try to guess what she's thinking, feeling, etcetera, and see if she responds to me? This endless stream of questions kept running through my head as I considered the best way to approach her. Finally, I decided to let go of my own expectations and see what would happen. I reminded myself that I could not *make* a student trust me—first, it was my responsibility to show her I could be trusted. I chose to show up and meet her at her starting point. With each opportunity to connect, I engaged her with warmth, energy, and support. During individual sessions with her friends, I included her in the conversation, letting her know she was not expected to respond unless she felt comfortable. I included her in our small group counseling sessions but gave her the space to opt out of the activities. When I let Hannah take the lead, I started to see change. We were building trust but progress was slow.

Although I was willing to be patient, many of her teachers were not. Despite my attempts to educate them about Hannah's needs, some refused to accept that her condition was "real." They viewed her behavior as defiant and disrespectful, that she was "choosing" when, where, and with whom she would talk. In my heart, I believed her teachers cared about her—they just misunderstood her. They were feeling frustrated, hopeless, and unsure about how to help her; it is natural to redirect blame when one feels hopeless. Reflecting on it now, I wish I would have advocated and educated more with teachers. Knowledge is power and some knowledge is difficult to understand when it is outside of one's own experience. Yet there were a few teachers who went out of their way to support Hannah. When I shared my belief that relationships were important to Hannah, they listened and made efforts to build a relationship with her. When I explained how Hannah's anxiety manifested in the classroom, they provided alternate solutions for her. These teachers set aside their frustrations with and assumptions about her in order to let her know, in their small ways, that she mattered. And it worked. Hannah's performance and homework completion improved in classes where she felt valued. She started to communicate with me in small ways. She was participating because the significance of positive relationships was essential for her. She still could not articulate the importance of relationships to her or connect it to her success in certain classes. It seemed that Hannah's anxiety prevented her from deeply reflecting on her own thoughts and feelings. Or perhaps she had grown used to others speaking for her. Whatever the reasons, it seemed like Hannah was resisting.

Resistance occurs in counseling relationships when the client feels pressured by the counselor and pushes back (Egan, 2007). So many times I wondered, "why is she resisting?" Hannah seemed unwilling to try anything to improve her situation. If she was failing classes, we discussed strategies to get her back on track. We created homework routines that allowed for snacks, breaks, and rewards. She spent time "creating" this routine with me and then quietly "pushing back" by not implementing it. So we would move on to the next issue and try something different. Looking back, I should have proceeded more slowly and with more intention. Some of it had to do with my position: there was one of me for more than four hundred students, and there was always someone in need. I also feel it was inexperience and my own urge to be everything to everyone. My commitment to "prioritize my students' needs before everything else" was a double-edged sword. By doing so, I struggled to set boundaries around my time and tasks with students, which in turn caused me to neglect myself and my own self-care. Lunch? Who eats lunch unless you're eating with kids in your office? I was unable to be proactive because I was always running from one crisis to the next. Like the domino effect, one thing impacts another. My daily "hair-on-fire" experience prevented me from slowing down and really listening to Hannah. I could not truly examine what was and wasn't working in her homework routine because I did not ask the deeper questions. Although I was asking solution-focused questions—What is new or different from last week? What makes it different for you? What would you like to see instead of the problem? Who would you notice if the problem disappeared? How would it be different?—I was trying to solve Hannah's problems with my solutions. And I was perceiving her unwillingness to follow through as resistance. However, I had forgotten that solution-focused counseling rejects the notion of resistance. Steve de Shazer (1984, as cited in Bannink, 2006) argued the counselor's view of resistance tactics are actually authentic ways the client chooses to participate in the process. It is the client's way of letting the counselor know the solutions provided are not aligned with how the client does things. If I had taken the time to ask deeper questions, I would have more fully understood Hannah and I would have been able to better see the solutions she identified, as well as what motivated her. When I asked Hannah what her best hopes for graduation were, it was the first time I truly realized her fear about being left behind. I knew her goal was to graduate but I did not understand why it was important to her. It was only when I came alongside her and listened that we were able to make progress and identify Hannah's solutions.

Working with Hannah provided me with many lessons that I still carry with me today. First, without relationships, no real progress can occur. Humans are wired to connect to each other and need positive relationships to grow. Hannah showed me the power of relationships and the impact they can have on a student's growth, learning, and achievement. Second, being present and taking the time to listen in order to understand is when the magic happens. Finally, using the core principles of solution-focused counseling as a guide allows one to develop cooperative counseling relationships in which solutions can be identified and change can happen. Winston Churchill (as cited in Bannink, 2006) said, "The pessimist sees difficulty in every opportunity. The optimist sees the opportunity in every difficulty." Always the optimist, I view my students' struggles as opportunities—anything is possible because Hannah showed me it is.

DISCUSSION QUESTIONS

1. If you had a student like Hannah, what strategies would you use to build a relationship with her? What strategies would you avoid?
2. How would you work with teachers to best support Hannah in the classroom? What academic interventions would you try?
3. How can you utilize the solution-focused approach to address students' mental health needs?
4. According to de Shazer, "only a small change is needed." How would you help your students recognize the small changes?
5. The scaling technique can be a powerful tool to use with students. How do you envision using this technique as a school counselor?

REFERENCES

Bannink, F. (2006). *1001 Solution-focused questions* (2nd ed.). New York, NY: W. W. Norton.
Corey, G. (2005). *Theory and practice of counseling & psychotherapy* (7th ed.). Belmont, CA: Brooks/Cole—Thomson Learning.

Egan, G. (2007). *The skilled helper: A problem-management and opportunity-development approach to helping* (8th ed.). Belmont, CA: Thomson Higher Education.

Payne, R. (2008). *Nine powerful practices.* Retrieved from www.ascd.org/publications/educational-leadership/apr08/vol65/num07/Nine-Powerful-Practices.aspx.

Siegel, D. (2013). *Brainstorm: The power and purpose of the teenage brain* [Kindle Paperwhite version].

Part VI

Clinical Supervision: Discrimination Model

Supervision is an opportunity to bring someone back to their own mind, to show them how good they can be.

—Nancy Kline

For the final chapter of this book, clinical supervision was included as a "bonus" chapter. As many readers may be starting or finishing their practicum and internship experiences, please utilize this chapter to start conversations about the supervisory relationship. As you will read in this chapter, it is important that the supervisory relationship is collaborative and open.

Bernard's discrimination model was chosen to explain this relationship as it explores the three roles that the supervisor may utilize: teacher, counselor, and consultant. The supervisor moves through the three roles to address the three focus areas of skills: process, conceptualization, and personalization issues. In this chapter, the supervisor chooses interventions geared at the needs of the supervisee instead of the school counselor's own preferences and learning style. Finally, as you read, explore the role of the university supervisor and how that impacts the on-site supervisory relationship and adds yet another layer of supervision.

Chapter Sixteen

Katie

Supervisee: Katie Martindale is a twenty-four-year-old biracial school counselor intern. Katie's career goal is to become a school counselor at the high school level. However, she was unable to attain placement at a high school and thus completed her practicum in a primary school setting. Having encountered difficulties at her practicum site, she decided to seek a different placement for her internship. Katie is now beginning an internship at Ravenwood Middle School, where she has been assigned a new supervisor.

Supervisor: Andrea Baker is a forty-three-year-old Caucasian who has been a practicing school counselor at Ravenwood Middle School for twelve years and has served previously as a supervisor for four interning school counselors. Counselors at her school work on a rotating schedule, and this year her charge of students is in eighth grade.

University internship coordinator: Dr. Heather Anders is a thirty-five-year-old professor of counseling who has been in charge of her university's school counseling internship program for the past five years.

Setting: Ravenwood is a suburban middle school in the midwestern United States. The school hosts a student body of about one thousand, of which 80 percent is Caucasian, 15 percent black, 3 percent Asian, and 2 percent biracial. Sixty percent of the students are recipients of free or reduced lunches.

As you read this case study, look for the following:

- Potential confidentiality concerns
- Setting appropriate boundaries on the part of the counselor and the supervisee
- Ways to improve communication skills between the supervisor and the university internship coordinator and the supervisor and the supervisee

- Supervisor changing her role to that of supervision in the discrimination model approach
- Supervisee's lack of confidence and dependence on the supervisor

CASE STUDY INTRODUCTION

The following scenario illustrates issues regarding confidentiality, setting appropriate boundaries, and the necessity of good communication skills in addressing both needs and concerns. While reading this case, keep in mind that the supervisee's previous experience had been in the elementary setting and she was now in a middle school. The supervisor, having successfully ushered four previous students through the internship process, felt confident in her role. The supervisor utilizes Bernard's discrimination model for supervision and her counseling is strongly influenced by the Rogerian person-centered approach along with interventions from solution-focused brief therapy (SFBT).

INCIDENT

It was early August, just prior to the start of school, when I received a request from my principal to take on an intern for the upcoming school year. Having successfully guided four students through their internships in the past, I had decided that, although it was short notice, I would be able to get a plan in place for my new intern with little trouble. Shortly after agreeing to accept this new charge, I received a phone call from the university internship coordinator, Dr. Anders. Because I had not supervised for this university before, I did not know Dr. Anders, though I found her to be a quite friendly and rather fast-speaking woman. She provided me with a short introduction to the program and explained "what it meant to be a supervisor." Toward the end of this conversation, she asked me if I had any questions. Feeling confident in my role, I assured her that I had no questions. At that point, she informed me that I would be receiving the standard biweekly emails to check on the progress of the intern and that an electronic version of the internship manual would be forthcoming and thanked me, somewhat profusely, for taking on this responsibility on such short notice.

A few days later I received a phone call from Katie, my new intern. She informed me that she was eager to start her new internship but would not be able to begin until the second week of school. She provided no explanation for her late start, but I assumed she had her reasons, so I simply told her that I looked forward to meeting her and assured her that we would have a great school year.

It was the second Monday morning of the school year when Katie arrived in the doorway of my office. She struck me as a cheerful young woman and appeared to be enthusiastic about starting her internship at Ravenwood. We had an hour before the school day started, and as was my custom with interns, I opted to use that time to start our scheduled supervision hour. My office is quite spacious (a luxury in the school counseling world), and in the center of the room I have a large round table, which normally plays host to group sessions. I asked Katie to join me at the table and she obliged, taking the seat next to me so that we could speak more easily.

I opened the conversation, "We're glad to have you here at Ravenwood. Now, I suppose before we discuss anything else, your faculty coordinator informed me that we need to complete a learning contract?"

Katie, somewhat surprised, asked, "Oh, you've already spoken to Dr. Anders?"

I nodded, adding, "Yes, she contacted me at the beginning of the month."

"Oh," Katie said, "Yes, I need to turn in an assignment that outlines our supervision plan."

At this point, I took the opportunity to inform Katie about my supervision style. "We are going to schedule our supervision every Monday before the students arrive here at the middle school. For the sake of supervision, I want you to know that I will be utilizing the discrimination model. What I like about this model is that it provides me with some flexibility and allows the supervisor to meet interns where they're at. There will be times when I am more in the teaching role and will be teaching you about school counseling, giving direct instruction. There will also be times when I am in the counselor role, where we will look at things like case conceptualizations. Hopefully, by the end of the experience, I will be mostly in the consultant role, where you will be bouncing ideas off me as a colleague. As you gain experience and self-confidence, I will primarily be in the consultant role."

As I continued my explanation of expectations, I noticed that Katie seemed more fidgety than other interns I had supervised. I could tell that she was paying attention to what I was saying, but she seemed nervous and kept averting her gaze to the floor or the door. Although I felt certain that Katie was, indeed, paying attention, it is vital to the discrimination model that I gain a clear understanding of where my supervisee is in the moment. I prompted, "I know this was a lot of information. Do you have any questions about what I expect?"

Hesitantly, Katie shook her head no.

I followed up, "Do you have any concerns about the internship?"

"Well," Katie brushed some stray hairs from her forehead, "I am a little nervous working with this age group. I've always seen myself working with older students, but I've never had that opportunity. But I do have siblings this age, and they think I am the 'cool' big sister, so I kind of get them. After all, I have had to put up with many sleepovers."

I nodded politely, making a mental note that I may be in the teacher and counselor roles a bit longer than I had anticipated.

Affirming her feelings, I said, "I can understand your apprehension since you've had most of your experience with second graders. You will see, though, that developmentally and cognitively these two age groups are extremely different. Do you foresee any specific skill areas that you would like to work on as you make this transition?"

I was surprised when Katie shrugged and replied, "Not really. I just hope that I can relate and connect with them." After a pause, she went on to say, "If I had to name something it would be interpersonal skills." My previous supervisees had replied to such questions with a great deal more insight into the challenges they might face and the skill deficiencies they would like to address.

It was at this point that I decided to provide my new intern with a bit of encouragement. "You will have lots of opportunities to build rapport and connect with the students. For instance, we will be in the eighth-grade hallway each morning where you and I will welcome the students. As you get to know the students, you can have quick check-ins with them before the bell rings. We will also have cafeteria duty each day. Although we are officially 'monitoring,' I often like to use this time to get to know the students better."

The remainder of our conversation that morning focused primarily on other clerical matters. When I looked at the clock and saw that our hour was almost up, I suggested, "It's about time for students to arrive. Why don't we walk up to the eighth-grade hallway and greet the students as they go to their lockers?"

Katie responded with a broad smile indicating that she liked the idea, and she followed me into the hallway. As I was engaged in saying my hellos to some of my eighth graders, I heard a voice a little further down the hallway exclaim, "Hey, Big Dawg! I didn't know you went here!"

Startled, I turned to see what the commotion was. It was Katie. She was addressing one of my eighth graders named Dante. Dante had been a "frequent flyer" in my office during the past two years, with an aptitude for both football and for frequently getting himself into trouble. Dante shouted back, "Hey, Kay-Kay, what up?" Katie then approached Dante with arms extended and gripped him in a playful bear hug in the middle of the hallway.

As the students made their way to their classrooms and Katie and I were left alone, I took the opportunity to inquire about the exchange. "Katie, it appears that you know Dante. Is he a relative?" Katie smiled and said casually, "Oh no, but he might as well be. He's one of my brother's best friends. He hangs out at my house quite a bit, especially in the summer." Upon hearing this, I knew I had to discuss with her further the importance of professional boundaries.

As Katie and I made our way back down the hall, I asked her if we could talk further in the office. She was agreeable and I led Katie to the round table.

I began, "Katie, I didn't think about mentioning this at first, so I apologize for that. In a school this size, it is not uncommon that you may know someone." Katie nodded as if agreeing. "Obviously," I continued, "you seem to know Dante very well. Why do you think it would be important to treat someone that you know in the same way you would treat other students?"

Katie hesitated as she adjusted in her chair and looked away. "Well, I guess it might be taken by some students in the wrong way. Like, I may play favorites. I remember teachers like that."

Being aware of the need to make sure that my intern felt heard and validated, I replied, "Yes, that is one reason, and it's part of a bigger picture. As a school counselor, you need to remember to maintain professional boundaries." I realized at this point that I needed to be in the teacher role for supervision. I took a moment to explain professional boundaries as I saw them applying to her in the situation. I felt confident that Katie was both attentive and receptive to my instruction.

Later that day, Katie and I made our way to the cafeteria for the eighth-grade lunch period. I explained to Katie that this was an excellent opportunity to mingle with students, observe, and make connections. As I was walking around, I noticed Katie talking to a table of boys. I was surprised to hear the students laughing and beginning to ooh and aah. I quickly walked over to the table to investigate the commotion. The students were still laughing but when they noticed me approaching, they began to motion to each other to quiet down and said, with a coyness that fooled no one, "Good afternoon, Mrs. Baker!" This is when I noticed Dante was one of the boys at the table. As I was about to ask what the commotion was, the bell rang and the boys quickly left the table to go to their classes.

Later that day, when I was once again alone with Katie, I inquired about the incident. "Katie, I noticed that there was a bit of commotion at lunch right before the bell rang. The reason I walked over was to see if I could assist in any way. Was everything OK?"

Katie answered casually, "Oh, that was just Dante being Dante. He asked me how old I was, which he already knew, but I reminded him anyway. And then, one of his friends was like, 'Do you like younger guys?' But don't worry, I told them, 'Of course not.'"

At that exact moment Katie's phone rang, at which point she raised a finger as if to say, *just a minute*, and she took the call. I was glad that phone call had occurred, because I was truly in need of a moment to contemplate my next course of action.

When Katie had completed her phone call, she put her phone back in her pocket, looked up at me, and said, "Hey, that was my brother. He needs me to go pick him up. Is it cool if I just head out a bit early?"

I nodded my consent. Once Katie had left the room, I took a deep breath and sipped my afternoon coffee. I decided that I would focus my thoughts on Katie later and instead went about the routine of checking my emails before the close of the school day. While perusing my inbox, I noticed a message from Katie's university internship coordinator, Dr. Anders. It was a standardized message checking in to see if I had any concerns about Katie or if I was in need of any assistance that Dr. Anders could provide.

I felt quite conflicted as to whether to share the day's events and my concerns about them with Dr. Anders. I decided that my best course of action would not be to voice my concerns just yet but to continue to work with Katie and attempt to make clearer to her the importance of professional boundaries. That decision made, I sent a quick note to Dr. Anders indicating that I had no concerns and that we had a good first day. I must admit that after I pressed "send," I cringed to myself at my lack of truthfulness. Today had been far from a "good" first day.

Despite my best efforts and lengthy explanations, Katie continued to struggle in the areas of appropriate boundaries and professionalism in the weeks that followed. Most of her transgressions centered around Dante. For example, on one occasion, she announced, within earshot of other students, that she would catch Dante later at the soccer game. On another occasion, she handed Dante money so that he could get extras at lunch, again in the presence of other students.

Each time I addressed the situation, Katie appeared to understand the importance of maintaining a level of professionalism so that her role was clearly defined to all members of the school community. Yet her transgressions continued.

I finally reached my breaking point when I overheard two of my teacher colleagues jokingly bantering with one another about the seemingly strange nature of the relationship between Dante and the new school counseling intern. I had to take action. I sent an email to Dr. Anders that afternoon informing her that there were issues that I would like to discuss with her concerning Katie during our upcoming site visit. Before the day was through, I received a reply from Dr. Anders informing me that whenever a site supervisor expresses a concern, she liked to meet with them right away so that the matter can be addressed as soon as possible. I was glad to have heard back so promptly and we scheduled a meeting for the following Monday.

I welcomed Dr. Anders to my office and led her to a seat at the round table. I started the meeting by informing Dr. Anders about all of the good qualities I had seen in Katie. I mentioned her sense of ease with classroom guidance lessons, her pleasant and helpful demeanor, and her willingness to listen to feedback. I then broached the topic of my concerns with Katie's professional boundaries and her seeming inability to learn from my feedback.

"When did you first notice this issue with boundaries?" Dr. Anders inquired.

I hesitated for a moment and then decided to be blunt, "Unfortunately, from the first day." I went on to explain the situation, "I found out on the first day that she knew one of my students on a personal level. Katie's brother is close friends with a student of mine named Dante." I then explained to Dr. Anders the incidents that had occurred that first day and recounted the events that had transpired in the intervening weeks.

Dr. Anders chimed in, "This is very interesting. She never mentioned any of this in class."

I went on to explain that I had attempted interventions with Katie on numerous occasions and that each time she seemed receptive to the feedback I was providing, but ultimately I would see no change in her behavior. Dr. Anders listened intently to my account of the situation. By the time I had finished telling her about all the action I had already taken, I began to feel a bit embarrassed that I had not reached out earlier.

As though sensing my embarrassment, Dr. Anders asked, "I'm curious if you felt it necessary to make so many interventions, why did you not reach out to me sooner? All of your emails have indicated that things were going just fine."

I wasn't quite sure what to say, but I answered honestly, "Well, at the time I felt confident that Katie would heed my feedback. She was very attentive during our discussions and seemed receptive to what I was telling her." I thought for a moment and then added, "You know, I also just didn't feel comfortable bothering you with something I thought I should be handling. I've had four supervisees in the past, and I've never had this kind of problem. I use the discrimination model in my supervision, and I know that the teaching role is an important aspect of this approach. I was hoping to give her a chance to turn things around and I was afraid I might lose her trust by reporting these incidents to you. It seemed important to maintain her trust so that we could move out of the teaching phase of the model."

Dr. Anders nodded in understanding. She told me that she could understand my apprehension and my reasoning. Then she offered, "You mentioned that you've had several supervisees and never encountered this kind of problem. It is such a difficult thing, knowing when it's time to reach out for help. This is a question that I often ask my supervisors to help them gauge their feelings about their supervisee: if you were asked to write a letter of recommendation for this supervisee right now, could you?"

I wasn't sure where she was going with this, but again I answered honestly. "The answer would have to be an emphatic no."

Dr. Anders then advised, "I have to say, I appreciate your honesty. The fact that you would have such a hard time seeing yourself writing a recommendation for this supervisee is an indication that it may be a good idea to reach out for assistance. It can be a hard call, I know. I know you don't want it to come off like you're 'telling on' Katie, but our role, when it comes down to it, is to be gatekeepers. We can do this best when we are working together. For instance, if I had been told about the first incident, I could have been a consultant for you and given you suggestions on working with this particular student. It's also on Katie, too. If she would have shared with me *her* concerns and told me about your interventions, I would have contacted you, and we could have been having this conversation sooner. At this point, though, I feel the best step forward is to mediate this situation with you and Katie and establish a clear understanding of the problem. Then we can develop a plan of action together. We will want our plan of action to be clear and agreed upon by all three of us so that Katie can, hopefully, have the opportunity to demonstrate growth and conclude her internship successfully."

For the next forty-five minutes, Dr. Anders and I went about the task of developing a plan of action. She helped me to articulate the kind of progress I would need to see from Katie in order to write her a quality letter of recommendation and feel comfortable in signing off on her internship. I found this exercise very helpful; together we were able to come up with a list of skill sets that we believed Katie could improve upon. By the end of our meeting I felt confident that we had identified the areas of improvement that would be most beneficial to Katie and that I would be able to explain this to her, clearly articulating my expectations.

The following day, Dr. Anders and I met with Katie in my office. I opened the meeting with a friendly, "Hi, Katie! I know you may be surprised to see Dr. Anders here. I've invited her to join our meeting so we can discuss your progress up to this point. I shared with Dr. Anders some of my concerns about your relationship with Dante, and she felt it was best that we all met together. I know this is difficult and may be uncomfortable for you, but I want you to be assured that we both see your strengths and want to give you the opportunity to grow in the areas of concern."

Katie's face suddenly became flushed and she appeared embarrassed.

Dr. Anders injected, "Katie, we meet every other week for class and much of our time is used to discuss any concerns at your sites. I was surprised that you never mentioned any difficulty. I assure you that we can work through this, but we need you to be honest and take responsibility."

This is when I noticed that Katie's eyes were beginning to well up with tears. I handed her a tissue, as I assumed the counselor role in the discrimination model.

I asked, "Katie, can you please tell us what it is like for you hearing this feedback?" Katie seemed a bit uncomfortable and appeared to search for words. She began to stammer but then was able to say, "I just feel like a failure. I think I was just trying to handle it on my own because I didn't want to look like I didn't know what I was doing. I've been having a hard time separating my personal and professional lives. I'm really sorry."

At this time, Dr. Anders and I looked at each other, both of us seeming to know that although Katie required considerable remediation, she was now ready to take responsibility. Together, Dr. Anders and I explained to Katie that regardless of any interpersonal relationships we may have, we have an ethical duty to the profession and to all of our students to maintain appropriate professional boundaries.

We then invited Katie to join us in constructing a remediation plan, outlining the areas that needed improvement and the steps that would be taken to make that improvement. The plan included the standard acknowledgment that completion of the steps outlined was required in order for Katie to successfully fulfill the internship requirement and that failure to do so would result in delaying her graduation with the possibility of additional remediation or even dismissal from the program. Dr. Anders explained that although delayed graduation and dismissal from the program were undesirable outcomes, they were necessary potential outcomes to enable Dr. Anders and I to fulfill our roles as gatekeepers, upholding the integrity of the profession. Dr. Anders informed both Katie and I that the implementation of the plan would require more regular monitoring of Katie's progress and that Dr. Anders and I would communicate about Katie's progress once a week until all stated goals had been achieved. Having been involved in the process and feeling confident about her level of understanding of the expectations, Katie signed the plan.

Over the next month, I observed Katie being much more conscientious in her interactions with Dante. Katie began asking more thoughtful questions and during our supervision times she was not only attentive but actively engaged. Most encouraging to me was the way that Katie embraced the process. Upon signing the plan, I was quite uncertain as to how Katie might react. I had been fearful that she might be resentful or defensive in our communications. This could not have been further from the truth. It was apparent that Katie had taken responsibility and was committed to her continued success, and she viewed Dr. Anders and I as invested participants in helping her to achieve it.

As the end of Katie's internship approached, I wrote to Dr. Anders informing her that our remediation plan was successful and I was happy to report that I would be writing Katie a positive evaluation *and* a strong letter of recommendation.

It was the Friday of Katie's last week when we met for our final supervision. Looking at Katie as she discussed her plans for the future, I was struck by the contrast between the Katie who sat in that chair the day Dr. Anders had come and the one who sat before me today. This Katie was possessed of confidence and maintained a humble pride in the fact that she had completed her remediation plan, knowing that she had truly grown.

When I told Katie that I had a letter of recommendation prepared for her, she thanked me graciously and I could see tears begin to well in her eyes, but being a professional, she maintained her composure. Katie and I reminisced about those early days of her internship. "I can't believe I was even like that," Katie admitted. I patted the table, and with great sincerity said, "You know what, Katie? Neither can I."

It was mere coincidence that as we were having our meeting that day, Dante happened to come bouncing around the corner of my office doorway. He had intended to enter, and before I could explain to him that we were in the middle of a meeting, Dante looked up and said, "Oh, I'm sorry for interrupting, Mrs. Baker and Miss Martindale. I'll come back later." As he was walking away, I looked at Katie and smiled. She had certainly established a professional status—even with Dante.

CASE DISCUSSION

In the above case, Bernard's discrimination model of supervision was utilized by the site supervisor. The discrimination model is an integrated model of supervision that offers flexibility for supervisors with regard to how they choose to interact with supervisees (Bernard, 1979). This model identifies three possible roles for the supervisor to take on during supervision (i.e., teacher, counselor, and consultant). There are also three foci for supervision that include interventions, conceptualization, and personalization. Together, these roles and foci give the supervisor nine possible ways to respond to a supervisee (three roles multiplied by three foci) (Bernard & Goodyear, 1998).

In this case, we saw the teacher role used in conjunction with the personalization foci when the site supervisor was discussing the role of professional boundaries. The site supervisor shifted into the counselor role and utilized the conceptualization foci when asking the supervisee to reflect on the implications the favoritism she was showing toward Dante may have had for other students. The site supervisor was acting in the teacher role by developing remediation requirements, as evaluation is a component of the teaching role. The role that the site supervisor did not get the opportunity to display during the case study was that of consultant, though it can be inferred that by the end of the internship experience she had been utilizing that role more often with Katie. By the end of the internship, the site supervisor would have been allowing the supervisee to share more responsibility and to be seen more as a resource.

Adherence to a supervision model provides a framework for helping supervisees to adhere to the American School Counseling Association (ASCA) national model and ethical standards while developing their counseling approaches. In the above case, the supervisor was forced to spend a more-than-ideal amount of time in the teaching role due to deficiencies in ethical boundaries and professionalism. It was important to prolong the teaching role because Katie needed encouragement and guidance to acknowledge her limitations.

An ethical consideration relevant to this case is addressed in the 2016 ASCA ethical codes, standard D.1, which maintains that supervisor concerns be communicated in a timely fashion to the university. Because these concerns were not communicated in a timely fashion, valuable time was lost and utilization of the consultant role was delayed.

Another relevant ethical consideration is seen in section D.M. of the ASCA ethical code, which states that the supervisor has the responsibility to assist in the initiation of remediation plans.

The case presented in this chapter illustrates three important aspects of the school counseling supervision process. First, it demonstrates the importance of timely and clear communication between the site supervisor and the university internship coordinator. Second, the case emphasizes that the supervisee is ultimately responsible for his or her own success and as such must communicate openly and honestly with the site supervisor and the university internship coordinator even about issues that may result in remediation. Third, remediation is, above all, an opportunity for growth, and though it is often viewed by students as a punishment, it is an important aspect of the gatekeeping process, ensuring that all practitioners are prepared to enter the school counseling profession confident in their competency.

We saw in this case that the site supervisor was hesitant to reach out to the university internship coordinator. Her hesitation was understandable. She was, after all, confident in her own ability to remediate the situation, and she didn't want to jeopardize the supervision relationship by making Katie feel as though she were being undermined. Having previously had only positive experiences with internship students, the site supervisor underestimated the degree to which the university internship coordinator could have been helpful to her. This is the primary reason that the Council for Accreditation of Counseling and Related Educational Programs (CACREP) requires the university internship coordinator to reach out to the site supervisor on a biweekly basis: to ensure that the site supervisor is continually made aware that the university internship coordinator is a resource to her. The site supervisor should have consulted with the university internship coordinator much earlier than she did. Upon realizing that her discussions with Katie were not being effective, she should have reached out for help. The site supervisor owes the supervisee ample time to remediate issues.

We also saw in this case a supervisee who was at first reluctant to take responsibility for her own growth. Katie had ample opportunity to receive suggestions and feedback during her internship class, which is mainly designed to provide a supportive space to discuss concerns. Having received so much intervention from her site supervisor, Katie should have been aware that she was having problems and should have sought input from the class instructor and peers. Katie also did herself a disservice by not communicating with her site supervisor her own concerns about her abilities up front. This is seen in the case during the development of the supervision learning contract. At that point, the site supervisor directed Katie to identify potential areas for her future growth, and Katie gave only a vague response. She did not engage in active reflection and therefore did not discover her true concerns about her own ability. Had she done so, the site supervisor could have been more mindful of those concerns while observing Katie and developed a means of assisting Katie in overcoming those particular areas of weakness.

Finally, we saw in this case a supervisee who embraced the remediation experience. Katie, as many students are inclined to do, could have chosen to view her remediation as a punishment. She could have opted to be defensive about her deficiencies or dismissive of the process, both of which would have inhibited her success. Instead, she was able to see remediation for what it truly is, an opportunity for growth. She was able to benefit from the feedback provided from both her site supervisor and the university internship coordinator, recognizing that they were working collectively on her behalf. In Katie's case, the remediation process worked as it is intended: deficiencies were identified, a plan of action was constructed, and growth was achieved as all three participants worked together toward a common goal.

DISCUSSION QUESTIONS

1. How would you describe the ideal relationship between the supervisee, the site supervisor, and the university internship coordinator?
2. In preparing to become a supervisee, what steps could you take to ensure that you receive the appropriate supervision and support?
3. Review the ASCA ethical codes section on supervision. In the case presented, what other ethical responsibilities may apply? How would understanding these ethical codes be useful to a supervisee?
4. Given the known facts of this case, what action items would you have included in the remediation plan?

REFERENCES

American School Counselor Association. (2012). The ASCA national model: A framework for school counseling programs (3rd ed.). Alexandria, VA: Author.

American School Counselor Association. (2016). Ethical standards for school counselors. Alexandria, VA: Author.

Bernard, J. (1979). Supervisor training: A discrimination model. *Counselor Education and Supervision, 19*, 60–68.

Bernard, J. M., & Goodyear, R. K. (1998). *Fundamentals of clinical supervision* (2nd ed.). Needham Heights, MA: Allyn & Bacon.

Council for Accreditation of Counseling and Related Educational Programs. (2016). CACREP 2016 Standards. Retrieved November 2, 2018 from https://www.cacrep.org/for-programs/2016-cacrep-standards.

Index

abuse, 18; sexual abuse, 121; witness to, 24
academics, 76; academic development, 100; self-development and, 11; support for, 130
accommodations, 18
acculturation, 72
achievement, 89; high-achievement, 133
acting out, 22
Adler, Alfred, 53
Adlerian theory, 47–56, 57; components of, 64; perspective and, 60; principles of, 63
administration, 92; values and, 123
adolescence, 157
adoption, 57
adversity, 30
advice, 21
advocacy, 18, 43; goals and, 113; learning and, 100
African Americans: experiences of, 39, 42; staff as, 36; students as, 33–34, 134
alternatives, 62
American School Counseling Association (ASCA), 12; guidance lessons by, 117–118; models from, 54, 88, 99–100, 113; recommendations by, 89
anger, 9, 92; attacks and, 106; control and, 95, 148; escalation of, 59, 93; goals and, 146; of students, 35
antidepressant, 21

anxiety, 17, 87; avoidance and, 26; diagnosis of, 18
appearance, 6, 7; hygiene and, 11; information and, 105
application, 113; family systems theory, 124; reorientation and, 74; of techniques, 77
approach, 67; considerations for, 126; family systems theory and, 129, 130; goals and, 16; solution-focused, 145
arrests, 119
ASCA. See American School Counseling Association
assumptions, 41, 42
attendance, 94; safety and, 109
attention, 93; to context, 63; power and, 49; responsibility and, 98
autobiography, 74
avoidance, 22, 23; anxiety and, 26; defiance and, 27; referrals for, 82; terminology and, 85

balance, 89
behaviors, 9, 124; clues about, 81; compulsions and, 17; disruption and, 92; escalation of, 93; evaluation of, 93; events and, 29; family and, 54; focus on, 94; goals and, 48; improvement and, 104; redirection of, 49; social-emotional learning and, 47; students and, 51; tracking of, 60; triggers for, 91

About the Editors and Contributors

Dr. **Marguerite Ohrtman** is an assistant professor, director of school counseling, and director of clinical training at the University of Minnesota's Counseling and Student Personnel Psychology program. She received her doctoral and master's degree in counselor education and supervision from Minnesota State University, Mankato. She is a former classroom teacher, a licensed school counselor in Minnesota, and a licensed professional counselor in Minnesota. In addition, Marguerite supervises counselors, counsels clients in private practice, and serves as a consultant to school districts. Marguerite is the president for the Minnesota State Counselor Association, former past president of the Lakes Area Counselor Association, and is active in many professional organizations including American Counseling Association (ACA), Association for Counselor Education and Supervision (ACES), American School Counselor Association (ASCA), and local counseling organizations. Marguerite has published and presented on several school counseling subjects, such as the achievement gap, the training and resiliency of school counselors, and technology in counseling. Marguerite Ohrtman wrote chapter 1, "Liam," and is a coeditor of this book.

Erika Heltner is a school counselor currently working in a middle school. She received her MEd in secondary education and school counseling from the University of Minnesota. Erika is a licensed/certified school counselor in Minnesota and Colorado, and she has worked as a school counselor at the elementary, middle, and high school levels. She is also working toward her professional clinical counseling license in Minnesota and works at a pediatric clinic providing counseling for children and families. She has presented on a number of school counseling topics including culturally responsive counseling, teenage anxiety, depression and suicide screening, and promoting self-esteem in teenage girls. Erika Heltner wrote chapter 2, "Sarah," and is a coeditor of this book.

* * *

Derek Francis is a high school counselor in the Twin Cities area. He grew up in the Minneapolis area and attended a suburban school, the school in which he currently works. Relationships with people, students in particular, are the foundational element of his practice as a school counselor. Derek believes in supporting students unconditionally and utilizes a person-centered, strengths-based approach in the school setting. Derek also believes in the importance of developing self-awareness in order to be an effective school counselor; he understands how self-awareness related to individual bias can benefit the student-counselor relationship, and he firmly believes in advocating for each and every one of his students.

Emily Colton has been a practicing school counselor for three years. She graduated from the Counseling and Student Personnel Psychology master's degree program at the University of Minnesota, Twin Cities, in 2016 and is a licensed school counselor through the Minnesota Department of Education. During the second year of her master's degree program, Emily completed five school-counseling internships, including two internships at the elementary level, two at the high school level, and one at the middle school level. She has coauthored two publications: "Perceptions of Effectiveness of School Counselors with Former Graduates in a TRIO College Program" in the *Journal of Applied Research on Children: Informing Policy for Children at Risk* and "School Counselor Technology Use and School-Family-Community Partnerships" in the *Journal of School Counseling*. She has presented five times at the Minnesota School Counselors Association annual conference and at various other locations, including Adler Graduate School and the Minnesota Educators Academy conference. Emily currently works as an elementary school counselor in Minnesota.

Dr. **Sarah Cronin** earned her PhD in educational psychology from the University of Minnesota. She is currently an assistant professor in Bemidji State University's psychology department, where she teaches aspiring helping professionals in the undergraduate setting. In the process of becoming a licensed psychologist, Sarah's research and academic work focused on student development. She has a variety of clinical, counselor educator, and research experiences. Clinically, she has served youth and emerging adults from ages five through twenty-two and is in continual pursuit of multicultural competent counseling. From providing child-centered play therapy for children with attachment disorders to short-term therapy for late adolescents and emerging adults in a generalist setting, Sarah's clinical experiences support her current work educating and providing services to college students. Sarah has been researching school counseling since 2015, with a special focus on the impact of school counseling caseloads and its relationship to student outcomes. This research helps her understand the effects that educational policy and the environment have on the day-to-day school counseling work with students.

Carolyn Berger is an assistant professor for University of Minnesota's Counseling and Student Personnel Psychology program. She received her PhD, MEd, and EdS in counselor education from University of Florida. Carolyn is a licensed/certified school counselor in Minnesota and Florida. She has served as a school counselor at both the middle and high school levels. She is also a licensed professional counselor in Minnesota. Carolyn has published and presented on a number of school counseling topics including career counseling, postsecondary and career readiness, group counseling, and meeting the needs of students with chronic illness. Carolyn is actively involved in professional associations including ACA, ASCA, ACES, and state-level counseling organizations.

Brittany Pensis received her bachelor's degree in psychology and human development from the University of Wisconsin, Green Bay, and master's degree in counseling with a school counseling emphasis from Lakeland College in Wisconsin. Brittany has worked as a professional school counselor for eight years in Wisconsin and Minnesota in elementary, middle school, and high school settings and has completed training in trauma-sensitive schools, yoga, and mindfulness, positive behavior interventions and supports, and data coaching and analysis, which she incorporates into her school counseling practice. Currently, Brittany has her licensed professional counselor (LPC) certification and lives in Wisconsin with her husband Tyler and children Grace, Delaney, and Asher.

Susan Benigni Landis has been a school counselor for more than twenty-five years, working with students at all grade levels in both urban and suburban schools. Her formal education includes a master's of education in counselor education and school counseling, elementary and secondary education certifications, NBCC and LPC credentials, and a dual bachelor's degree in fine arts and psychology. She has held leadership positions in her state school counselors association as middle school chairperson and elementary–middle school sharing room facilitator. Seeing the job of the school counselor as creative and highly diversified, she has presented parenting workshops, staff training, and camp programs for students. She believes in the school counselor's role to teach skills for effective living and learning so that each child can experience academic as well as social success.

Dr. **Diana L. Wildermuth**, NCC, LPC, is an assistant professor and school counseling coordinator in the psychological studies in the education department at Temple University. Previously, she was a high school counselor and counseling department chairperson in a southeastern Pennsylvania for fifteen years.

Alicia Cobb is an incoming second-year MEd school counseling student who is completing her internship experience in an urban school setting. She currently works as a literacy instructor for high school students at a major university in an effort to bridge a gap between large universities and the residential communities that surround them.

Elizabeth Ferraro taught middle school for two years in an urban setting in Jacksonville, Florida, through Teach for America and has also completed a year-long school counseling internship in an urban high school setting in Philadelphia, Pennsylvania.

Mark Gillen, PhD, is professor and department chair in the Counseling and School Psychology Department at the University of Wisconsin, River Falls. During his thirty-four years of counseling, he has worked as an elementary and middle school counselor, day treatment counselor with middle school students in the justice system, and adventure therapist.

Gary Campbell is a practicing school counselor with twenty years of experience. Gary worked in the treatment foster care system for ten years before returning to complete his master's degree in school counseling from the University of Wisconsin, Stout. He presents at the Wisconsin School Counselor Association (WSCA) conference, has served on the WSCA board in a variety of positions, and is co-chair of the WSCA Conference Committee.

Olin Morrison is a practicing school counselor with seven years of experience. Prior to this he worked with organizations that served youths for more than fifteen years. He holds master's degrees in school counseling and educational leadership from the University of Wisconsin, River Falls. He has worked as a school counselor at both the elementary and middle school level and has served as chair of the Wisconsin School Counselor Association Board of Directors.

Laura Keogh is a middle school counselor in the Twin Cities area. She is a native Minnesotan, growing up in a small town outside of the cities until relocating to Minneapolis to attend the University of Minnesota. There she earned her bachelor's degree in child psychology and her master's degree in counseling. She found her passion working with middle school students as both a school counselor and a volleyball coach. In her work, she utilizes person-centered, family systems, and solution-focused approaches and supports data-based school counseling practices. Laura continues to seek out professional development opportunities in order to stay up to date on the latest research and practices concerning school counselors and educators.

Juli Montgomery-Riess, MA, served as a school counselor to students and families in both urban and rural sixth- through twelfth-grade schools in the Midwest for the past ten years. During this time, she also served as a counselor educator at the University of Minnesota and the University of Wisconsin, River Falls. From 2011 to 2018, she held a LPCC from the Minnesota Board of Behavioral Health. Juli currently lives with her husband and three children on their vegetable farm in Amery, Wisconsin, where she is the student success coordinator for the middle and high schools. She is passionate about comprehensive programming, systemic change, closing the achievement gap, and working cross-culturally to regain trust with students and families who have a history of school disruption and adverse childhood experiences. She utilizes trauma-sensitive practices with students, families, and staff in working toward school and postsecondary/career success.

Nicole Pierce-Risvold is a licensed school counselor who for the last seven years has been working with a variety of students. From elementary school students to high school students, including high-risk students who were flagged to drop out, Nicole was assigned to counsel students on personal, social, and emotional issues. She also holds a clinical licensure, LPCC, in which she works with children and young adult women. She currently is under supervision and practicing privately in the Twin Cities.

Jason Ferkinhoff and **Erin Kelly** are licensed school counselors in a Twin Cities suburban middle school where they and their school counseling team utilize solution-focused theory. Erin and Jason have presented on the application of solution-focused theory in schools at both the Minnesota School Counselors Association Conference and the Wisconsin School Counselors Association Conference and both are graduates of the University of Wisconsin, River Falls, counseling program.

Sarah Kortuem attended Minnesota State University, Mankato, where she earned her master's in counseling student personnel with an emphasis in school counseling. She began her career as a licensed professional school counselor in 2009 and has worked primarily at the secondary level. Sarah became a school counselor because she wanted her students to be seen, to be heard, and to know that they matter; she has been working to fulfill that vision through her work. She enjoys seeing the growth that occurs in students as they progress through their educational careers. She has a fundamental belief that it is her professional responsibility to maximize a student's learning potential and eliminate barriers to student success. She relies heavily on collaboration with colleagues, as their feedback provides a more complete picture of each student. In addition, she strongly believes that building positive relationships with students and families can bridge the gap between school and home. Highlights from her career include her previous role as the Lakes Area Counselors Association president, her current role as the president of Minnesota School Counselor Association, as well as the opportunity to be a teaching specialist at the University of Minnesota for the Counseling and Student Personnel Psychology program.

Carrie VanMeter is a licensed professional school counselor and licensed professional clinical counselor. She is a counselor educator who has served as the school counseling coordinator at her university for eight years. The role of school counseling coordinator may go by a different name depending on the university, but the responsibilities are the same. The school counseling coordinator is responsible for overseeing the counseling students' internship experiences from start to finish. This role typically involves assisting students as they find a placement that fulfills school requirements, developing a relationship with the site supervisors, and performing site visits and maintaining regular communication with the site supervisor to ensure adequate progress of the internship student. It is important for the school counseling intern to practice honest and open communication with both their site supervisor and the school counseling coordinator, as both are instrumental in ensuring that interns attain the skills necessary to be successful school counselors.

Terri Simmons is a licensed professional school counselor as well as a licensed professional clinical counselor with a supervisor credential. She has worked eight years in public education as a teacher and nineteen years as a school counselor. She also teaches the school counseling internship class at a local university. In addition, she is in private practice as a licensed professional clinical counselor where she specializes in children, adolescents, and families. She also is certified in trauma counseling. As a school counselor Terri has served as supervisor for numerous school counseling interns.